The Outlaw Preac

By: John Andrews

ISBN: 978-0-9856412-3-8

www.theoutlawpreacher.com

I would like to recognize and thank the following people (these people are real) for encouragement and assistance: Chris Wheeler for another awesome book cover, Jami Carpenter for patient and professional editing. The Prophets MC of Southern California, my wife DeEtt and my sons Tyler and Nolan for their love and unconditional support. My daughter-in-law Melissa for her encouragement, my adorable grandchildren Ella, Bria and Asher who support me even though they don't know why. My sister Laurie and my parents, James and Eleanor Andrews for their lifelong support.

The Outlaw Preacher and "The Miracle" are the first two books in The Outlaw Preacher series. Many thanks to the thousands of readers who have made The Outlaw Preacher a top 5 book on Amazon in the Inspirational category, your great reviews and fellowship have been a blessing I didn't expect. Please visit: www.theoutlawpreacher.com and join the crew.

CHAPTER ONE

It took a few rings before James realized it was *his* phone ringing. He had recently upgraded phones and the ringtone was only one of a multitude of confusing aspects of this new device. He loved technology but with the attention span of a hyper five-year-old, it was always a challenge to learn the workings of a new 'toy.'

"Hello," he answered.

"Nine Ball?" the voice asked.

"Yeah," he said, acknowledging his former street name with the notorious Doomsayers Motorcycle Club, known as the DMC by law enforcement and the outlaw biker world. "It's Spaniard, bro. Snake went down late last night — it's pretty bad. Thought you should know."

In a world of high speed violence James was quite accustomed to these phone calls. Guys were constantly getting stabbed or shot or mangled in motorcycle accidents, but hearing 'Snake's' name brought him out of the ether. "No way, bro; what happened? Where is he?" he asked, still shaking the fog from his early morning wakeup call.

"Loma Linda. He had emergency surgery. We don't know anything except he got hurt bad, there's swelling in his brain, and they're not giving us much hope right now," Spaniard said.

Spaniard succeeded Snake as the DMC Mother Chapter President or 'P' in biker lexicon. Snake had moved up to become DMC's National 'P,' had been one of the charter members of the club, and was an outlaw legend on the West Coast. It was Snake who buffered what could have been a storm when after the club had thrown an epic party welcoming him back from a three-year prison term and a one-year parole that allowed for no affiliation with the club, James aka "Nine Ball" abruptly retired from the DMC.

Unbeknownst to the DMC 's 416 patch holders, Snake had offered Nine Ball a prominent position as the club's National Rep to handle all negotiations as the club expanded into uncharted waters. It was a 'to die for' spot filled with all the power, money, drugs, booze, and women any outlaw biker could want, but God had other plans for James, and Snake, being an eyewitness to some crazy God stuff earlier that night had allowed

James to walk from the club in an unprecedented display of grace just six short months ago.

It was a private matter and only Snake's stature had prevented James from recrimination then and in the following months when he became a member of the Prophets motorcycle club.

"I'll pray for him," was all James could think to say.

"I figured you would, bro," Spaniard said.

"Hey Nine?"

"Yeah," he answered.

"Me and you are cool. I know what went down that night. Snake filled me in, but some of the brothers still ain't okay with you leaving and going with the Prophets. No disrespect to your club—we hold the Prophets up; I'm just sayin'."

A silent pause and then, "If Snake ... well, if he don't pull through, I just ... well, just be careful brother. I'll do what I can, but ..."

"Hey, I know the drill, bro. I appreciate you saying it, but I will trust God and see what happens. I know what I did for the club; you and I both know what time it is," James shot back, feeling that old rage coming for him again. "I'm trying to move on from that place, bro; I'm trying to forget what won't forget me."

"Hey, I'm just callin' to let you know. I don't need to get into old business with you; I'll see you around." The phone went dead.

Cell phones don't 'click' like the old phones. You can't really get a good "screw you," hang up anymore. Are you supposed to throw your four hundred dollar phone against the wall every time you want to hang up on someone? I think not. James sat for a minute staring at the 'call ended' display before terminating his side of the conversation. "Snake went down," he whispered out loud and in the same breath; "something ain't right."

Like James, Snake was a rider of riders, a man born to ride a Harley. Some guys go through years of riding before reaching a level of expertise that allows relatively safe high speed pack riding, if that's even possible. These two were naturals from the cradle.

Nine Ball and Snake rode like the wind. They rode as one. James had been Snake's Road Captain, the most trusted position on two wheels. The sergeant-at-arms took care of the 'P' while kickstands were down, but it was the Road Captain who ran the show when they were 'up' and rolling. James took a few minutes to think about the years of side-by-side adventures and then reached for his Bible for his morning reading. He prayed long and hard for his friend, ending his prayer as always with …"your will Lord, that's all I want."

It didn't take long for word to travel. Email made the biker world smaller but news had always moved quickly in this subculture, especially when it was bad. James started to get text messages from everywhere. Under Snake's leadership, the DMC had gone from a rowdy bunch of beer drinking motorcycle riders to a top ten ranked outlaw motorcycle club. A dubious honor, but one the DMC coveted and worked to advance.

Without Snake, this group could degenerate into a fractured bunch of hoodlums trying to establish control. Snake was no cult leader, but his 6'7" frame and sharp mind commanded a presence and not just anyone would be able to assume his position. It would be impossible. Had he not walked away from all of it, James would have been the likely successor. Now there were a bunch of lieutenants and no general. Not good for the general population and not good for James.

Snake was his unofficial cover and it was gone now. They would circle the wagons in a show of respect, but half a dozen power mad lunatics would be planning the overthrow. It was like a third world dictatorship and the 'P' was in a coma.

James collected his thoughts and made a call to his new 'P,' Kit. "Hey bro, it's James; don't know if you heard but Snake went down this morning. I don't have any details except that he's at Loma Linda. I want to see him, but need your counsel on how to proceed."

"No way," Kit exclaimed. "That sucks, bro. Snake's a good brother; we've been having some fun over there since he started showing up at church. But don't go to the hospital just yet; I'll call some of the guys and call you back. Keep praying!" Kit ordered, and then hung up.

What is it with guys hanging up on me today? James thought. The phone kept ringing for the next couple of hours and he sent all calls to voicemail. That's what it was for. He was waiting impatiently for Kit to call him back, unaccustomed to waiting for permission to move. He had been a "shot caller" for years and the humbling he was enduring as a new member of a club, which was light years away from the old life, was excruciating at times. He was learning patience and humility and it sucked! He loved the guys, the ministry, the newness, but having to start from below bottom was the hardest thing he'd ever done.

Just six months ago he'd been honored as a conquering hero at the Badlands party, the world at his feet. He'd had everything an outlaw biker could ask for and laid it all down to become a prospect with a Christian motorcycle club one twentieth the size of the Doomsayers. He humbled himself and earned his patch in three month and was more at peace than ever before, though the outlaw world laughed at him and that's a *big* world. He had a hundred enemies he never made but they were enemies nonetheless.

The devil is a patient dude and he's relentless in his pursuit of a target. James had a target tattooed to his soul. He was standing on the rock that is Jesus the risen Christ. The Bible calls it a peace, which passes all understanding. It would have to be.

CHAPTER TWO

As nice as Loma Linda University Medical Center is, it was still a hospital and nobody hated these places more than James did. He'd lost too many loved ones in them, none more painful than his wife Michelle a dozen years before. It felt like last month. He placed his cell phone in the front pocket of his Prophets MC cut but not before rendering it soundless by employing the vibration mode. He was still waiting to hear from Kit but knew the 'P' was a busy guy and maybe just hadn't had time to call yet.

Snake's real name was Richard Vandermere and he was currently in ICU-Recovery on the fifth floor. Only immediate family was allowed. *"Immediate family and the family pastor,"* James thought to himself. The elevator opened at the fifth floor and he followed the arrows on the wall toward the Post Op recovery wing, his Bible at his side. It was strangely quiet up there that day. Every other time he'd been there it was bustling with all manner of medical personnel, and visitors — aimless, awed, and terrified, though they pretended otherwise.

He passed some windowed double doors and saw two sheriff deputies drinking coffee at the foot of a portable bed. *Figures*, he thought. Another twenty feet and another double door, this one was controlled by the faceless ICU nurses behind the intercom. He pushed the button and waited.

"Can I help you?" came the voice.

"Vandermere; I'm his pastor," James said. It wasn't a really a lie, Snake had been attending his church on a sporadic basis lately. The doors opened inward, which was a blessing; had they been engineered differently, James' face was within striking distance. He made his way to the desk where he was met with several suspicious glares.

"*You're* his pastor?" the most courageous nurse asked him.

"Yes, James Walters," he responded in a dignified tone.

"521, last door on the right. He has visitors and he's only been out of surgery for a couple of hours, so he's not conscious," she said.

"Thanks," and he walked toward the room.

James recognized one of the patch holders as 'Bones' but didn't recognize the bigger guy. He nodded to Bones, but before he could say anything the big guy spoke up.

"What are *you* doing here?" he asked as he stood from the chair.

"Preacher, Prophets MC Mother Chapter," James announced as he extended his hand toward the biker.

"I know who you are, jerkoff; I said 'what are you doing here,'" he growled. James glanced quickly at Bones who was making no effort to mitigate this situation.

"I come in peace, bro; I just wanted to see Snake and pray for him," James said calmly, although he could taste the bile rising in his throat.

"If he ever comes around, I'll be sure to tell him. Now take your little Bible and get out of here before you need a room yourself."

"What's up, Bones? Your memory fading … you getting old … you forget his leash?" James asked. The big man lunged for James.

"You stinking punk — ahh my knee," the big guy screamed as James crushed it with one side kick and then drove his heel up into the big biker's nose, dropping him to all fours. Bones took a step toward James and was met with a roundhouse kick square in the jaw, depositing him on his back next to his buddy.

A third Doomsayer casually rounded the corner drying his hands on a paper towel and stood behind his two fallen comrades.

"Whassup, Nine? There a problem?" the massive bearded sergeant-at-arms asked.

"'Sup, Magic. We had a misunderstanding about visiting hours is all," James replied.

"I see that," he smiled and shook his head slowly. I see you've met 'Cedar.'

"We hadn't been formally introduced, but he seemed to know me," James answered.

"Well, he knows you now," Magic laughed.

"This ain't over, Preacher," Cedar said somewhat muffled.

"Shut up, idiot; you just let a guy with a Bible kick your butt," Magic said and continued. "Damn bro, you're serious about all of this, huh? I'm gonna have to come to your church more often; I know Snake was diggin' it."

"You are always welcome, bro; all the brothers are encouraged to attend. It's an honor to have you," James answered.

"You never know," said Magic. "You should split now, though; I'll get word to you when we know something."

It took the deputies about twenty seconds to find the trouble spot, draw their weapons, and order everyone on the floor. Cedar had a tough time of it; his left knee wouldn't cooperate.

"What happened here?" a deputy asked him as he wiped the blood from his face. "I smashed my nose opening the door," he answered.

"I see. And you?" He turned to Bones with an *I can't wait to hear this* look.

"Ah, well, when he hit his nose, his hand kinda came up and caught me in the jaw," he answered.

"Darndest thing," nodded James.

"I got here after it happened so I guess that's the story," Magic offered.

"Well, if that's it, I'll be leaving; please call me when he's conscious," James said to Magic. "Get some ice for that, keep pressure," James said to Cedar as he turned and walked toward the exit.

*****

As temporarily satisfied as he felt, James knew two things … three, actually. One, this wasn't over and two, he had straight up disobeyed his president's orders to stay put and it was the second thing that was bothering James the most. The third thing was he had strained his left hamstring on the roundhouse kick. Age was rearing its ugly head.

As he cleared the massive automatic glass doors, he pulled the cell phone from his cut. He took a deep breath and called Kit, noticing flowers of stunning yellows and purples bordering the circular drive and the breeze coaxing the giant palm trees back and forth against the royal blue sky as he waited. Kit answered after two rings. Voicemail was like cops—never around when you needed them.

"Yeah, hey bro; it's Preacher," James said, gathering his courage.

"Yeah, how's Snake? You hear anything?" he asked.

"Yeah ... no ... I didn't hear anything more regarding his condition just yet, that's why I'm calling, bro. I screwed up; I know that now, but I didn't wait for your call. I went to the hospital. I don't know why I did; I apologize," James stammered. He was about to enter a bad place.

"I see. Well, not much we can do about that now, is there? I guess it doesn't matter what I FREAKING say not to do; is that how it is, Preacher — or is it still Nine

Ball — you still think you're the shot caller? This ain't the FREAKING DMC; this is the Prophets. Maybe I took it too easy on you 'cause I thought you understood but you don't understand anything!" Kit ripped into him some more; "You want to run your own program, fine with me, but you ain't doin' it wearing our patch! You got that? You came to us, we didn't come to you, so you make up your mind. I don't want to hear anything right now. Read First Samuel chapter 13 starting at verse 8 and call me when you're done."

The phone went dead. *Jeez, another hang up; nobody says goodbye anymore,* James thought. He felt like a little kid who had been scolded by his big brother. It hurt his pride, but mostly it hurt because he had made the tactical error of using his friendship with Kit against the hierarchy of the club. Sure they were friends, great friends, but Kit was the 'P' and with that title came the responsibility to judge rightly and no soldier had the right to question the order of a superior officer. Kit was a great guy, funny and warm at times, but he knew his responsibilities before the Lord as the leader of his men. James knew that he had betrayed the trust he'd built over the months. The first thought that went through his thick skull was, *forget this, I don't need this crap, I don't need this stupid little Christian club,* but he had the remnant of sense bouncing around in his head that told him the sooner he located First Samuel, the better things would be.

James limped over to a large tree and slid to a seated position and opened his Bible to the suggested passage. *This is great, how the heck did he know to direct me to this?* he thought. *I'm the pastor here and this guy tells me what time it is? I've obviously underestimated my Prez,* he continued.

> *The Prophet Samuel had told Saul to wait seven days for him to show up so that he could offer the burnt offering to the Lord. Well, stuff started to fall apart for old Saul; seven days rolled by and no Sam, so Saul panicked and lit the offering himself. Not good. Sam showed up and asked what happened and Saul started trippin' all over saying, "you didn't show up when you*

said you would, the people were scattering, the Philistines were assembling, and I thought they were bringin' some war my way and I hadn't sought the favor of the Lord, so I lit it up myself," or something close to that. Like Kit, Samuel had ripped into his guy saying, "You did foolishly; you have not kept the command of the Lord your God." Dig this part: "For then the Lord would have established your kingdom over Israel forever! But now your kingdom will not continue. The Lord has sought out a man after his own heart, and the Lord has commanded him to be prince over his people because you have not kept what the Lord has commanded."

Now that was heavy. James was reeling from the direct hit on his pride. He wanted action; he'd always been a man who got things done, he'd always been a leader, and now he was forced, voluntarily, but forced to wait on the Lord instead of jumping off full steam in some direction — any direction — just do something! He had much to learn. He wasn't sure he could ever reach the level of humility required to be a great man of God, but deep in his spirit he knew he was called.

He picked up his cell phone and pushed redial. As Kit answered, James panicked briefly, remembering that Kit hadn't told him where to stop reading. *Oh, this is ridiculous,* he thought.

"Hey, it's me Saul," James said. Relief washed over him hearing Kit laugh.

"Very good, bro; that was good. We okay now?" Kit asked.

"I am if you are, brother. I get the message, I'm not good at this, but I'll keep trying."

"None of us are. I never told you this, but I prospected for a whole year about twenty years ago. I always thought I knew what was right but I learned that the strongest thing you can do is wait on the Lord. It doesn't seem like it, the world will make you second- and third-guess yourself all the time but the Lord is the only sure thing, so wait for Him. He will never leave you nor forsake you, bro; we are all in this together.

Now you see why we don't have four hundred guys."

"No kidding. I'll tell you what, bro, the DMC is deep in numbers but they are shallow in leadership. If Snake doesn't pull through — God forbid — I'm praying hard for him, but if he shoots through, that club will explode. It'll be like Iraq over there. Nobody can trust anyone; it'll be an epic power struggle. I hate to think what will happen," James said.

"There's something that's really trippin me up, bro," he continued.

"What's that?" Kit asked.

"I was five minutes from being the National Rep for the DMC. I would have had a legitimate shot at National 'P' in light of this thing with Snake. I don't regret what I chose to do, but it is kinda weird." There was silence on the other end of the phone line. "You there?" James asked.

"Yeah, just thinking about what you said; very heavy stuff, for sure. You will have to remain strong, Preacher. Your church is growing, the Lord has huge things for you, the warfare will be intense, so just watch out. It might not be so easy next time, there might be more than two."

James was stunned. How the heck did Kit know what happened upstairs thirty minutes ago? "How did you ..."

"Never mind how, just know that I know," Kit replied. "I'll see you at church tomorrow night, brother. As far as Snake is concerned, you'll know when you're needed. Wait to be called; don't just volunteer," Kit said as he hung up.

CHAPTER THREE

Early summer in Southern California provides some of the best motorcycle weather in the world. Saturday mornings were his personal favorite. Years of random insanity had given way to at least one reliable-as-clockwork activity, the Saturday morning ride. His method of operation was to rise early, don his leathers, and run the hill to Big Bear City and enjoy a long breakfast on a wood deck overlooking the main drag in town. There he could write a sermon, which thus far had rocked his now two hundred person congregation every Saturday night. He had a way of taking the truth of scripture and weaving it into street level daily life and his growing following was soaking it up every week.

James pulled the strap on a brand new full-faced helmet that had been a recent gift from Linda. He had to try it at least once before he tossed it into the corner of the shop in favor of his reliable piece of crap novelty helmet, the fit of which he had become accustomed. James was always a careful rider with Linda aboard, but she'd heard far too many stories of his high speed antics to hope he was that cautious when alone. She would never come between James and his bike. She feared the outcome of that tactical move. But if she couldn't slow her man down, she could at least mitigate the risk. He'd wear the full face today.

The beauty of the Harley Davidson Street Glide, besides the excellent power band and comfortable ride, was the stylish hard saddlebags that could hold chaps, gloves, an extra helmet, leather jackets, and on Saturdays, his laptop computer. He easily slid the device in the left side bag, as most of the other items were employed on this brisk early morning. The chaps would go into the bags first, then the jacket, and finally the gloves, as temperatures were projected to rise from the forties to seventy-five in Big Bear City later in the day. For now, he was wrapped like a Chipotle burrito.

He pushed the start button and smiled as the big bike roared to life. There was no better sound anywhere. With almost fifty thousand miles on her now, she still ran like a Swiss watch.

***

For the uninitiated, the smell of acres of orange blossoms is intoxicating to the point of distraction. Many mountain road trips were delayed by unplanned stops in the middle of this nearly two-mile sensory immersion. James slowed his roll through the aromatic highway and lifted his face shield to welcome the smell. He thought that heaven must smell like this. He hoped so. He took the opportunity to thank God for allowing him to enjoy this quiet euphoric ride and asked that he be given wisdom and insight necessary to communicate His word to the crowd tonight.

The orange blossoms gave way to a pleasant cool moist air that tasted great and served as a wakeup blast, filling James with vigor and clarity. As he rode along the highway, he prayed for his friend Snake and offered him to the Lord. James believed a couple of things: one was that God had a bigger plan for Snake and two, God was in control and it was His will that this servant sought. His prayer ended with, "Thy will be done."

A mid-seventies model Chevy pickup pulled up next to James as he sat at the only stop light between him and a rollicking mountain ride. He was a sucker for old Detroit pickup trucks.

"I like your truck," he yelled through his half-opened face shield.

Two skinhead-looking guys in their late twenties just nodded. The passenger said, "Nice day for a ride; be careful out there."

James just nodded and looked ahead. The light changed and as usual the bike got away first. He watched the pickup truck fade into a dot in his mirror. He moved in his seat to find that perfect spot where he would navigate the familiar but no less exhilarating ride ahead. He pulled over with the intention of removing his leather chaps, but as he sat idling, changed his mind. There would be some cold pockets on the way. He could just as easily take them off at the top of the hill. The older James got the less he enjoyed freezing on a ride.

The time spent in indecision gave the Chevy a chance to catch up to him and he allowed the truck to pass before he pulled onto the highway. He ran through four gears and figured he'd overtake the truck once and that would be the end of it. The last long straight section would give him ample opportunity and he was gaining fast. He noticed the rear window of the pickup truck was slid open, probably to enjoy the breeze flowing through the cab.

As James downshifted and readied himself for the move to the left, he looked at his speedometer, which was dead on fifty miles an hour. He twisted his hand, looked ahead, and saw nothing but straight deserted highway. This would be fun. Then in slow motion, he saw the truck slow and the passenger lay the barrel of a shotgun onto the back window ledge and then, a flash. His mind played a tape of his drill sergeant telling his platoon that in battle, you never hear the shot that kills you. If he heard anything it was his front tire exploding and the forks and fairing of his bike folding into the asphalt at fifty miles an hour. "Oh God, save me!" was all he remembered until he was standing in the middle of the road with both arms raised like a referee presiding over a winning field goal.

James had slid and flown and tumbled several times before landing on his feet, arms raised, laughing as his demolished motorcycle lay a hundred feet behind him. He was laughing. Like a crazy man. Laughing and praising the God of the universe. In the seconds following the attempt on his life that had claimed his bike, the ritual of his morning armor assembly played in his head. There was the leather jacket, not the cotton hoodie; the gloves and chaps were afterthoughts ostensibly to fight the chill of the morning. Last but not least was the decision to wear the gift helmet instead of the toy that would have disintegrated upon impact and with it, his head.

God had orchestrated his choice of attire this morning; how cool was that? James would not be visiting Big Bear City today but he had his sermon. Ephesians chapter 6, "Put on the whole armor of God," which dealt with spiritual warfare, of course, but the physical manifestations of spiritual attacks would strike a collective chord in the congregation. The shotgun would not be mentioned, at least not tonight. It was a front tire blowout. That was the story to which he would stick. It would drive his enemies crazy. He walked to the side of the road and called Kit. He would need a trailer.

***

The second phone call was to Knucklehead Jim at the local Harley dealer. Jim's faithful attendance on Saturday nights was about to net him a sale. He placed an order for the floor model 2012 black Street Glide that he had spied a week earlier during a visit for parts and synthetic lubricant. The deal was struck over the phone with a promise of $4,000 cash down. Knucklehead assured him that the loan approval would only take thirty minutes and he could pick up the bike later in the day, absolutely before church that evening.

The makeshift plan was to throw whatever settlement the insurance company paid directly at the loan, which would leave him eight to ten months worth of payments to pay it off. He hadn't planned on buying a new bike, but on occasion circumstances dictated alternative action. His trained eye determined that his bike would be a total loss so he quickly determined there was no reason to wait.

He had an alternative motive as well, get back up as fast as possible and be seen riding around town within twenty-four hours of the assassination attempt. He thought it was a good witness to the power of God. Plus it would drive whoever was behind this to insanity.

He called a Prophet brother to ask about the next biker swap meet in Long Beach. It was the next day. He laughed once again at God's timing and provision. There were several leather items that were in need of replacement after surfing the asphalt. He would be better than new by the next afternoon, betrayed only by the small cuts on his face where the twelve-gauge shot had managed to fill the void left by the half-opened facemask. These could easily be explained away by flying gravel during one of his several summersaults.

The Prophets loved to be the first guys at the swap meet gate at 6 a.m. This was problematic for James as his propensity to stay up late and play pool after church made the early morning a challenge. He resigned to set the alarm and quit whining.

He would have to call Bud and borrow the truck he'd sold him just after his release from prison a few months back. He shook his head and smiled. He really shouldn't have sold that truck.

Thank God for cell phones; his was ringing again. Kit had called Bud, who was now calling James. "What happened out there; you okay?" Bud asked.

"Yeah, I'm okay, a bit scratched up but praise God, it could have been much worse," he answered.

"I'm on my way out. I'm gonna stop and grab the trailer but I'll be there as soon as I can. I'm glad you're not hurt, James; that could have really screwed up tonight's service," Bud said laughing.

"Appreciate your concern, buddy; see you when you get here."

One thing for sure, he was blessed with a group of quality friends. The one phone call he dreaded was next on his list. Linda would overreact and push every button he had, all in the name of love. James gathered his wits and decided that he would act like he appreciated the concern and accept that she only freaked out because she loved him. Why that was he still couldn't figure, but she was crazy about him and he really did enjoy that part. He was, as his friend Brian had noted, "over-chicked." A drop dead gorgeous professional woman in love with a scruffy old biker — go figure. He smiled and pushed her number. He wasn't *that* old.

"I knew something was wrong! I knew it," She spoke loudly, almost yelling, but James let it slide.

"Look baby, I'm fine; it was a freak thing, but hey, I was wearing that full face you bought me and it saved me," he answered in a feeble attempt to avert the wrath by spotlighting the positive.

"Dang it, James, I'm sorry. I just get so scared that I'm going to lose you on that thing," she said.

"I hear you, baby, but God's got it all under control. I'm seeing that more today than ever," he said. "I'll be back at the shop in a couple hours; I'll call you then. I love you, babe."

"Okay, I love you, too. Just quit scaring me!" she said.

"Hey, look on the bright side, I get a brand new bike out of the deal. That's pretty cool, huh? ... Babe?"

She hung up. *Guess she's speechless; must be excited about the new 'Glide,* he laughed. He was a bit of a jerk, but a lovable one.

CHAPTER FOUR

Tom Petty said it best: "The waiting is the hardest part." James was learning patience, but it was an excruciatingly slow process. He'd determined that waiting for something, especially when he was alone, meant he would have to face himself. It was not pleasant.

Much had been revealed in the short time James had been walking with the Lord. He'd learned that his addiction to music was just another tactic to avoid 'alone' time. He still enjoyed music, but now made it a habit to spend some quiet time every day just meditating and praying. This was no easy task for an adrenaline junkie! And now, since his motorcycle stereo was smashed, he was forced to sit and wait for Bud in total silence. He thought about singing, but that would be cruel to any nearby animals or birds. He begrudgingly sat on a rock and waited. In silence. *How the heck could he and Snake both wreck their bikes in the same two-day period after tens of thousands of miles together without incident?* he wondered. His initial thought when Spaniard first called was that something wasn't right. After facing the business end of a twelve-gauge shotgun, he was beginning to harbor a conspiratorial inkling or two.

He could almost understand why someone tried to off him, but Snake? That was insanity. Snake was the kingpin of what was arguably the most notorious outlaw motorcycle club on the West Coast. You didn't just walk up to this guy; he was protected almost twenty-four hours a day. If — and it was a big if — someone got to him, then there were huge questions, unacceptable breaches with internal security.

Magic seemed extremely calm at the hospital, especially considering the fact that James had embarrassed two of his club brothers. He could have crushed James, technically and literally. He had every right to 'put the boots to him,' and as quick and ruthless as ol' Nine Ball could be, he was no match for Magic. No, there was a reason Magic was the sergeant-at-arms. He could destroy a small town on his own. There were legendary tales of violence bearing Magic's signature. Magic had joined the DMC just a couple of years after James aka 'Nine Ball,' had participated in several old school brawls alongside Magic, and had witnessed many others. That was not a fight that he wanted. Not now, not ten years ago, not ever, thank you very much. So there was that … while his 'P' lay in intensive care and his brothers were getting their butts kicked in the hallway. Maybe knowing it was just Nine Ball, there was nothing to worry about, nobody was gonna get beat up too badly.

Looking back it just seemed weird. It made no sense that Magic would be involved in anything treasonous; he was a down brother, DMC through and through. No, it had to be someone, something else, something stunk; James wanted details and answers to questions surrounding the 'accident' that had knocked the biggest man in his life on his back with a dozen tubes dictating his life function. James prayed again for guidance and wisdom and that God would heal Snake and bring him to a saving knowledge of Jesus Christ. As sure as he was that something beyond an accident was at work here, he had a feeling deep in his spirit that God had a much bigger plan for Snake than to slowly die in that hospital bed.

***

Bud and James pulled the twisted metal from the trailer and unceremoniously dropped it behind the dealership as instructed. The magnificent machine had been reduced to scrap metal in the blink of an eye. James philosophized about life being that way for people. He'd certainly seen his share of tragic endings. *Life is so fragile, Christ is eternal.* Perspective was everything. He'd need to keep that in mind when ignoring his fiancée when she voiced her concerns about his lifestyle. He was too quick to tell her, "That's who I am, it's who I was when you fell in love with me, deal with it." That might all be true but he was determined to convey his message in a more loving manner. Such growth.

He'd been alone for many years and was hesitant to love completely; his trust had been betrayed before and the memory of that pain bridled his passion. Since his wife, Linda was the first woman to pursue him through his tough guy veneer and it had him excited and nervous. Time would tell. They planned to marry in six months. He wanted a year and she wanted three months. It was their first compromise.

Knucklehead was true to his word. All James needed to put his leg over the 2012 Street Glide was a signature and four grand. He provided both. Bud insisted on taking a few pictures. James rolled his eyes and said, "Really? Bud, you want pictures? You want them before and after I take off the training wheels?" Bud ignored his grumpy friend and documented the entire event with digital precision.

"You'll thank me later," he said.

***

James thanked his friend for the ride and the help. He had several hours before the seven p.m. service and his curiosity was killing him. He needed information about Snake's accident. Where … how … stuff like that was driving him nuts. He called Spaniard. As expected, the conversation was guarded and brief. James was able to learn only that Snake crashed on the mountain road near his house in Crestline. It was treacherous riding up there for sure, but Snake had rolled that highway twice a day for a dozen years. In the winter months, before and after the snow, the fog up there was hand-in-front-of-your-face thick. Snake and Nine occasionally raced up the hill in that fog, such was the awareness each had for every bend in that spastic highway. Spaniard gave him enough information to at least go take a look at the spot. He figured he could satisfy his curiosity by visiting the crash site. It would make a dandy first ride on the new bike. He had time.

CHAPTER FIVE

As familiar as Snake was with the mountain highway, James could be a close second. He had lived up there for several years and the daily commute was twelve miles of motorcycle riding bliss. Sweeping canyons and long stretches of straight smooth pavement made for a world-class run in San Bernardino county. The new bike sounded great. All of the first round performance improvements were already done by the dealer. He would have preferred to do them himself, but the bike was already tricked out so what the heck, any additional work that wouldn't void the warranty would be done at Inland Performance Systems by the owner himself. After a measured run up the hill he knew the ride stabilizers would be the first modification and that would be the very next day! The bike ran strong, but the big machine tended to 'hop' a bit on high speed corners and to this former outlaw that characteristic was unacceptable. He made a mental note to take care of that issue right away. There was no way he was going to alter his style of riding; the bike would have to adapt to him, not the other way around.

The sun was high but moving west so the visibility was excellent. James slowed as he approached the crash site, opting for a turn-out where he could safely park and then walk the hundred or so feet to where his friend had met a painful and abrupt ending to his evening ride. Per Magic, Snake had 'lost it' on a sweeping right turn, laid the bike down, and slid into the guard rail, which kept him from flying off the mountain. James had crashed into the same mountain about five miles farther up after a long afternoon of beer drinking some twelve years back, so he knew all about the respect that must be paid up here. Trouble was, Snake knew it as well and James just wasn't buying the story that Snake just 'lost it' on a turn.

He pulled into the turn-out and his foot found the kickstand and pushed it into the well-worn asphalt. He placed his helmet on the seat and took a long look at an old familiar area. It was one of the most peaceful places in Southern California. It could be fiercely lonely up here but it could provide some much-needed solace at times. James loved the sound of nothing but wind and he drank it all in for a few minutes. He thanked God for the time alone and began walking, his head down. He thought back to the episode of *Kung Fu* when Caine was finally able to snatch the pebble from the hand of Master Kan. "A wise man walks with his head bowed, humble like the dust." Master Kan rewarded his prize pupil with this sage wisdom as he bid him farewell. James shook his head, marveling at what his mind had chosen to remember and how a TV show from forty years ago had shaped much of his life's philosophy before Christ.

As he came upon the skid marks and debris that lingered beyond the county's effort at cleanup, James was sobered by the eerie feeling that this was where his friend lay broken a couple of days ago. The accident had occurred just before 10 p.m. when Snake was on his way to work at the railroad hub in San Bernardino. He'd worked the same 11 p.m. to 8 a.m. shift for five years, maybe more as James recalled. This only served to strengthen his conviction that Snake didn't just space out and lose control of his bike. He stopped and turned to look up the road and from this vantage point he saw a weird-looking patch in the road about thirty feet back up the highway. He headed back to take a look. This time he walked with his head up as several cars were winding their way toward him and after being shot at this morning, he was a bit jumpy. He laughed to himself as he thought Caine would also opt for this method. No wisdom in being flattened by a car if you could avoid it. James pressed against the mountain to allow the cars as much area as possible as they passed by.

He came upon a square of pavement that appeared darker than the rest of the highway. He removed his sunglasses to make sure. He looked up the road for additional traffic was headed his way. Another convoy of cars was coming down but he figured he had a minute or so before they got to him. He walked out to a spot just at the border of the square patch, and squatting down on his aching knees, dragged an index finger over the pavement. Oil. A perfect square spot on the highway reflected a fine coat of some kind of oil. It was a dark brown color and had a slick, sticky feel. If this stuff was on the road when Snake hit it on a sixty mile an hour sweeping right, it definitely caused the slide into the guard rail. How it got there in that perfect square pattern was another question.

No way anyone just poured oil there, not in a square, not that finely and evenly distributed. The only thing James could imagine was one of those trucks, which sprayed oil in an effort to minimize dust. He knew nothing about that industry but somehow the image of a truck applying a quick uniform blast of oil on the pavement just before Snake rolled through seemed like a possibility. He further reasoned that this substance might begin oily and slick and then cure with time, which explained the sticky feel it currently possessed.

Was this an attempt on Snake? Was it meant for someone else? Was it inadvertently sprayed on the highway and Snake was unlucky enough to ride by minutes afterward? *Yeah, sure.* This smelled of intent. He'd seen enough; someone had tried to kill Snake just like they tried to kill him this morning. Coincidence in the outlaw world didn't exist. If something seemed rotten, it probably was. James headed back to his bike; he had a sermon to preach and a couple of hours of preparation was in order. He liked to honor the scriptures by doing at least a little study and praying before imparting the most important information on the planet.

***

Seven p.m. on Saturday on the east side of San Bernardino was getting to be the happening side of town. A brightly lit warehouse sporting a ten foot black banner with white writing in a huge paint brush font said simply, *REAL CHURCH,* and somewhat smaller, 'Southern California' underneath. The parking lot filled up early with motorcycles and pickup trucks, luxury cars and clunkers. It was pretty much what he had envisioned sitting in his prison cell just two short years ago. God was faithful. If that was all he had learned, it was a lifetime of knowledge. If we would just believe and trust that statement, all the psychiatric drug manufacturers would close overnight.

The human condition is frail and becomes volatile and highly unstable when relying solely on its own wisdom to navigate the uncharted waters of personal relationships, which if you think about it, is the causal factor in all the violence in the world. We all just can't get along, Rodney. Proverbs chapter 3, verse 5 and 6 states, "Lean not on your own understanding, in all your ways acknowledge Him and He shall direct your paths." If God is faithful, then His word can be employed and if that happens ...

CHAPTER SIX

James loved his congregation and spent hours with all who would stay after church and fellowship upstairs in the Upper Room, named for the hangout in the book of Acts. This room was forty feet long and forty feet wide with a pool table dead center and plenty of seating throughout the fifties diner motif. Massive urns of coffee and iced tea, along with a plentiful supply of bottled water, greeted every visitor. It was all on the honor system, something James was warned against but was dead set on maintaining. Sure enough, the donations in the metal box fastened to the wall had always well exceeded the cost of providing refreshments. God was indeed faithful. James did put a small sign above the box that simply said, "Kick down, you cheap suckers; life ain't free!" Linda had cringed when he insisted on displaying the sign, but everyone else loved it. They loved his delivery; he was the same guy in the bike shop or the grocery store as he was at church. He loved them right back but his ritual was to sneak into the building and lock himself in his office that was adjacent to the upper room a couple of hours before service and just spend some quiet time with the Lord. He usually had a pretty good idea of the evening's topic and an outline of the sermon, but the finishing touches happened in this room and sometimes in the middle of the sermon!

His pre-game ritual consisted of equal parts Joe Bonamassa and other blues greats and his favorite Christian band, Third Day. This praise/blues groove was the greatest place to feel the Lord's guiding hand regarding the evening's teaching. The growing group of people who opted to stay later were treated to hours of this bluesy praise and worship groove and with it some great impromptu comedy.

The Prophets attended en masse, even though several of them also attended a Sunday morning service in Orange County, which was challenging after a night of coffee, tea, and games of pool and darts that went until 3 a.m. at times. They all agreed it was a better and safer alternative to their former Saturday nights. Several of the Doomsayers patch holders and even a couple of officers had been attending with increasing regularity as Snake was becoming a semi-regular.

James wondered how that patronage would hold up in light of Snake's current condition. It could go either way; either a bunch of them would be so concerned about their president's situation that they might feel inclined to rub their 'God' lamp for some good luck or nobody would come as the only reason they ever showed up was because Snake did. That was certainly true for Magic. He had to be there with his president; it would be interesting to see what happened next. James didn't worry much about it. He trusted God to bring who needed to be there; it was the way he started *Real Church* and it had worked out rather nicely thus far. He figured if it wasn't broken, don't try to fix it. His little church had grown from fifty-six people at the informal Bible study at Bria's house to over two hundred on Saturday night. Steady growth for a church that knew nothing of modern church growth techniques and would most likely react unfavorably to anyone trying such tactics. Lots of love here, but you wouldn't want to tick some of these people off; they weren't *that* saved!

The preacher kept it simple on Saturday nights. He knew he was dealing with multiple levels of spiritual maturity from the seeker to the twenty-year 'know it all.' He knew he was embarking on a touchy subject tonight with Ephesians chapter six, but he figured every believer or seeker would be faced with the reality of our enemy and his tactics of disrupting our lives through "spiritual warfare." That night would be as good a time as any to discuss it.

His office window provided a panoramic view of the front parking area, so he was able to judge attendance before he ascended the three steps to the rear of the stage from a back hallway below his office. James basically stayed away from the crowd until after the service. He wasn't completely anti-social, it just worked better for him to spend that time in prayer and light reading before running up on stage at the end of the last song. Several attempts were made to introduce 'live' music to *Real Church* on Saturday night, but James remained steadfast in his approach. There was top-notch contemporary Christian music playing at all times in the warehouse/sanctuary.

The sound crew consisted of Stewart, a nineteen-year-old pierced and tattooed kid who had been attending ever since the place opened. He had the job because he asked the preacher if he needed any help. James immediately put him in charge of production and volume. That was his only job. James submitted the playlist to Stew every Wednesday at the Men's Bible Study who gathered the music and built every service exactly as planned. The lyrics of several selections were projected onto a large screen and everyone sang along. James much preferred this method of corporate worship to dealing with the egos of a 'worship band.' Stew had a feel for the congregation, or 'congo' as he and James affectionately referred to the gathering, and masterfully orchestrated a great mix of music culminating in a loud "God of Wonders" by Third Day, which signaled to James that the time was near. When the preacher heard that song, he made for the stairway and timed his stage entry to the last twenty seconds or so of the song. That was as theatrical as it got but it never failed to gather and ready everyone for the evening's word.

"Praise the Lord!" James yelled into the wireless microphone that fit over his head with a thin and comfortable plastic band. He had become as dependent on this device as some public speakers are with their teleprompters. This preacher paced and wandered all over the stage as he brought the word of God to his audience. He tried a handheld microphone and felt caged. It had been the worst sermon ever, according to James. Linda noticed his discomfort, but no one else seemed to mind. To James, the preoccupation with the microphone was torture. After that night it was forever wireless. He was free to roam about the stage, which allowed him to interact with the people and each individual had the feeling that the preacher was speaking directly to him or her. He was moving slowly tonight, the roundhouse kick and the nasty fall having rendered him a bit sore and tight. He thought to himself that the next day would really hurt. Physically beat up, but spiritually and emotionally sky high.

"God is good; we need to live in the freedom of Christ and our spirits should be forever thankful," he began. "Wake up and smell the black coffee, no fufu latte cinnamon dolce sissy stuff, the coffee cherry, the good stuff; wake up and take a deep breath! Nothing is too much for our God. Amen?" The congo loudly agreed. James continued, "Check it out; sometimes bad things happen to us. I'm preachin to ya, you hear me; sometimes bad things happen to us, dig?"

"AMEN," they all yelled back.

"We live in a fallen world, man; it ain't gonna be perfect till He comes back. There is gonna be trouble; it ain't all pastel-colored balloons and rainbows when you receive Christ and His amazing gift of salvation. Do you hear me? Is anyone here tonight? Am I preachin' to myself?" Cheers of agreement filled the building.

"My friend Snake went down last night on highway eighteen out of Crestline. He's on life support at Loma Linda Hospital. Snake is a bad dude, a big dude, a leader of men and check it out, he's been coming to *Real Church* for a couple of months now; not every Saturday, but more and more he feels at home here and guess who ain't too happy about that?" James challenged. "The enemy the devil, that's who," he yelled out before anyone could answer. It was loud in there; people were shocked and saddened to hear about Snake, not that they knew him well but he was highly visible. His huge physical presence, sleeved arms and electric blue Harley with the twenty-one inch "ape hanger" handlebars were all hard to miss.

He was terrifying at first glance, but the folks who stayed late with the gang upstairs were becoming fans of the big man. His laugh and sense of humor were contagious and he was the only person who could give the preacher a decent challenge on the pool table. They had some epic best-of-sevens up there and the fan base for Snake was growing. James loved it. He knew that the Lord was doing some heavy work with Snake and to be an instrument in that process was humbling and exhilarating. It was precisely this type of ministry that James envisioned when he cleared the gates of Folsom prison eighteen months before.

"We need to pray for our brother Snake. I don't know that he's accepted the Lord, I don't know that he hasn't, but we need to come before the Lord and ask for a miracle. I don't know how to explain it to you other than to say that I just don't think God is finished with Snake yet," he said amidst loud "Amens" from the crowd. He led them in prayer. "Heavenly Father, we come before you tonight in thanksgiving and praise for who you are. We thank you that you loved us enough to send your only son as the perfect sacrifice for the sin of the world. We know that only Jesus Christ could fulfill prophecy and provide that perfect means of salvation. We know that no other approach to you, Father, is possible. We love you and thank you for your perfect plan.

"Tonight we are saddened by the injuries of our friend Snake and we ask you to heal him, Lord; we ask that you baffle and confound the medical professionals in that hospital who say there is no hope; we ask that you glorify your name in this miracle and that Snake will be healed and come to a saving knowledge of your son Jesus Christ. In all things we seek your will, accept your will, we trust your will, and we rest in your response. In the precious and matchless name above all names, our savior Jesus Christ, Amen." A resounding "Amen" echoed back at the preacher. His head remained bowed as he praised God for the love of these people.

He went on to preach like never before. He challenged his congo to rise up each day and as scripture admonishes, 'put on the whole armor of God, be ready for conflict, be ready to trust God for all things, be ready to be attacked but not to shrink from the battle. To trust God in all things was an ongoing commitment, not a one-time deal. It was not for the faint of spirit.'

As James led his people in closing prayer, he looked up and nodded to Stewart who hit the button and flooded the sanctuary with ZZ Top's "Jesus Just Left Chicago," which James insisted was a worship song. The party was on.

As he began to descend the steps to ground level he saw them approach. Magic and four DMC patch holders were making their way to the front. They were not smiling.

"Brother, thanks for coming," James extended his hand to the burly sergeant-at-arms.

"We need to talk; they're pulling the plug," Magic yelled over the din of the room.

"No! No, they can't; not yet," James yelled back. "Come with me," he said as he motioned to several

Prophets who were watching this exchange from the second row. Gambino, fresh from heart surgery but feeling better than ever, was the first brother to reach him.

"Bro, you know Magic," he said as they two men shook hands. Gambino nodded to the other DMC as James continued. "Here are the keys to the church; can you cover for me?" he asked. "I need to get to the hospital."

Gambino frowned. "Of course; you have to ask?" and grabbed the keys and motioned for the Prophets to follow him.

James Nine Ball turned to Magic and said, "Bro, with all respect, I didn't ask you ... is it okay for me to visit him?"

Magic peered with those dark eyes, framed by an even darker beard, and said, "That's why I came, but you better hurry. The place will be filling up, you won't have much time. I'll make sure you're not hassled," and gave him a neck squeeze, which told him they were okay ... for now.

CHAPTER SEVEN

His eyes searched for Linda. She was doing what she did best, talking to several ladies at one time and making them each feel like she was their best friend. She was a natural in her new role. She would be good for James and fantastic for the church. He moved to her and whispered that he had to roll to the hospital and for her to keep everything in prayer.

She pulled back and looked deeply into his eyes and said, "Go! I'll take care of everything here. I love you."

"Get with Gambino if you need anything. I'll call you as soon as I can. I love you, too. Magic!" he yelled. The big man turned. "Can I ride with you?"

"I don't know; can you?" Magic smiled for the first time that night.

"Oh yeah, I think so," James laughed.

"Let's go then; we're wasting time," the big man said as he nodded his head toward the exit.

With the five DMC in tow, James made his way as quickly as possible through the mass of people and out to the motorcycles. It was evident to everyone that this wasn't the night to ask for his time. James hated to blow everyone off, but he absolutely *had* to get to that hospital.

If Magic noticed that the bike next to him was a 2012 black Street Glide and not a 2006, he kept it to himself. James made a mental note to get with Magic regarding the events of the morning. He hadn't forgotten that someone had tried to blast him into heaven before his time, but at the moment, Snake's situation was a bit more pressing.

Riding with the Prophets MC was great, they rode tight and fast, but riding with a veteran Doomsayer was just plain mean. That old feeling was like a drug. The arrogance with which Magic rode was an assault on anyone in his way. He terrified motorists with his black beard and constant yelling as he tore through traffic, often kicking cars and side mirrors just to strike fear and ensure a safe passage for his crew and to hell with the citizens. James, or Nine Ball, as he'd become once again during the five-mile tear to the hospital, struggled with the mainline of adrenaline versus his unwillingness to terrify the general public at every turn.

That was his life just a few months ago; officially, he'd lost his 'edge' somewhere between the exit gates at Folsom and the day he met the Prophets. This was a cheap attempt from the enemy, a reminder of the power and prestige of the outlaw world in an effort to dissatisfy James in his current pastoral position. It didn't work. Yeah, it was a rush to ride like that again, but the thrill was gone. He was a new creation in Christ and he rested in the knowledge that he got the better end of the deal.

When they rolled into the hospital parking lot, surprisingly Magic slowed at the guard shack. But then he yelled something at the guard, jerked his bike around the speed bump, tore down the straight driveway to the entrance of the hospital, and parked his bike squarely against the red curb. The security guard only glanced at the small group of bikers lining up against the scarlet curb before quickly turning his head. He was obviously not interested in enforcing the ordinance, not for fourteen bucks an hour.

After a small conference, which excluded James, Magic sent the other patch holders upstairs. James felt the alienation but reminded himself that the Lord had said that the world would hate him because it first hated Jesus. It was comforting. The massive sergeant-at-arms turned to his former colleague and said, "Do whatever you gotta do up there, Preacher; you've got fifteen minutes." He nodded as he retrieved his travel Bible from the inside pocket of his Prophets cut. The two represented spiritual polarity at its finest. They would have made a great picture, the weathered and filthy old Doomsayers MC patch next to the months' old Prophets MC patch, its light gray lettering contrasting brightly against the black background. The old and the new, the flesh and the spirit.

It was actually pretty deep in a theological sense. James stopped and asked Magic the question that had been burning inside of him all day. "Did you green light me, bro?"

"The hell you talking about?" Magic snapped. "If I green lighted you, you wouldn't be here," he said as he turned and walked toward the hospital. Ninety percent satisfied, James followed without a word. They entered the elevator and Magic pushed the fourth floor button.

***

"You gonna heal him with your little Bible there, Preacher?" Cedar mocked.

"Hey Cedar, what's up. No, I ain't gonna do anything but bring it before the Lord," James responded with an amazing amount of grace and self control. His flesh wanted to snap this punk's neck, but he figured that would be a lousy witness. He also wanted to make mention of the metal strip taped to his nose but let that opportunity pass as well. He did stop and turn back to Cedar before entering Snake's room. "Cedar, you ever get up the Highland side goin' toward Big Bear, you should ride up that way sometime; it's a blast!"

Cedar looked at James and turned his head with a snicker, but said nothing.

Snake's room was as cold as it was sobering. The mechanical and methodical sounds of digital beeps and chirps blended with the blue, green, and red lights of the monitors which, to the trained eye, reflected the deteriorating condition of his big friend. To James, it was just noise; he didn't want to know what it all meant. After dealing with the loss of his wife and father, who both died in the hospital, James hated these places. He knew that medical professionals were highly trained and worked insane schedules in an effort to heal and care for all who sought their help. And though his mother died at her home when he was locked up, he was zero for two in hospitals; he hated to be there, not enough windows.

As his time was short, he opened his Bible to Psalms 23 and began to read out loud to his comatose friend. As he read the Psalm out loud, his voice boomed in the small room. Though there were only the two of them, he felt the presence of the Lord in a mighty way. It was during these mountain top experiences where God spoke to him through his obedience. Sure the Lord knew of his dislike for hospitals, yet he was uniquely qualified to split the defense and get to this room. Just as sure, God could heal Snake without his servant James in the room, but God was God and by that virtue, He can do as he wishes. His will be done. God's blessings extend to persons being used as a conduit, though it's not always clear how and why these things work. The obedient, the available very often receive the biggest ancillary blessings.

The preacher reached into his vest pocket and produced a small dark vial with a black screw top. He carefully placed a drop of the oil on his index finger and touched his friend on the center of his forehead. He was working without a net here; he'd read in the Bible that we are to anoint with oil and pray for healing. His job was to obey, in faith that God had him there for a purpose. He quietly asked the Lord to heal his friend and confound the doctors and that God's name be glorified through the miracle. He almost added that it would be nice if God didn't humiliate him by sending him in there in front of all those big bad mocking bikers, but he thought better of it. God wasn't missing any of this. He felt the twinge in his spirit that just said, "Believe and trust," so he did his best to believe and trust. His prayer was earnest and fervent; the Bible says that kind of prayer avails much. The enemy was already doing a tap dance on James' head. Doubt and despair were creeping in, terrifying thoughts of abandonment and loneliness, all flying in the face of God's promises, filling his head almost before he could finish his prayer and close the Bible.

He was sure that God wasn't finished with Snake. Was that just wishful thinking on his part? Why would he feel compelled to race over here to pray over his friend instead of taking the safe route and praying from church or at home? God could surely handle this without him. There he was with his Bible and his God in full view of his former club. He was the laughing stock of this subculture and it was easy to sit there and think, *No big deal, who cares what these idiots think of him*, but it was a heck of a lot tougher when those people were the only 'friends' he had for the past dozen years. Maybe this whole exercise was just to crush the last vestige of human pride that James had regarding the outlaw world. Maybe God was just finishing him off.

It sure looked that way right then as the two nurses who entered the room acted like he wasn't even there. They were talking quietly between themselves about the paperwork, the authorizations, the entire procedure, which is all it was to them, James thought. Just a procedure. They were more concerned about the hospital's liability than Snake's final minutes on this earth. James understood that this was the way of the world and they had to do their jobs correctly. He was just heartbroken that after forty-eight years nobody really cared about the final minutes of one Richard 'Snake' Vandermere. Well, almost nobody.

James loved his old biker friend; there weren't many like him left. It seemed that the younger more ruthless types were filling the ranks much faster than the old guys could impart the wisdom and 'class' of the lifestyle. The waiting room was filled with that type of guy. They were here because they had to be, not out of respect. James was struggling to be quiet; this was not his club any longer and he would be well served not to say a word.

All over Southern California, the older, wiser guys were stepping aside and letting the youth expand and conquer. It was much more dangerous this way. Back in the day a good war established pecking orders, hierarchies, and order in general. Treaties were honored and clubs were left to their territories with only the cops to worry about. Now, wars settled nothing. The young guns, unable to accept defeat or being "mud checked" (put in their place) by more established clubs and leadership, reacted like the spoiled children that many times they were.

One idiot with a big mouth could ruin years of trust. It was a gangland mentality and it was beneath the dignity of an outlaw. It sounds weird to say it like that but there was honor among thieves. The old outlaw James longed for the old days when he and Snake and others were underworld royalty with earned respect. A man's word and a club's charter meant something. The times, they are a changin'.

James walked back to Snake's side and held his hand surrounded by tubes running everywhere. He bent down to the bloodstained bandage and whispered into his ear, "Snake, it's Nine; I'm here, brother. Hey, you need to get better, bro; we have much to do for the Kingdom of God. You know that it was God who talked you into coming to my church. He has a plan for your life, brother, a big one, one you can't imagine. Jesus died for the sin of the world, bro; that includes you and me.

"You need only to ask for his resurrected life to take over your tore up life here, my brother. He died and rose from the grave so we could live in victory, but only if we ask him to take over our lives. We need to trust Him every step of the way; we can start tonight. He died for us so he could live in us and work through us. You need to get better, bro." Warm tears were slowly making their way down the old biker's weathered face. A couple of them landed on Snake's arm. James took a tissue from the generic box on the stainless table and patted his friend's arm. "Oh Lord, I don't know what to say, I don't know what else to do," he sobbed. "Why do you take the good ones and leave me with these other idiots?" he asked with a muffled laugh. There was that peace again. A flood of peace came over him and he took it for an answer. "He's all yours, Jesus; your will be done."

James gathered himself and prepared to meet the enemy in the form of Cedar and whoever else had amassed outside the door. Exit in victory; God is in control. He took a deep breath and opened the door.

CHAPTER EIGHT

The hallway was full of Doomsayers and supporters. James walked past several patch holders who just stared at him and continued walking to where Spaniard and Magic were standing just outside the waiting room, which was teeming with more DMC and friends. Evidently it was now *the* place to be. Magic was right; it filled up fast. James hated all of it and felt his old self surfacing; he knew he'd better get out of this place before bad things happened. It was after nine p.m.; surely visiting hours had to be over. He laughed to himself: *that would never stop the DMC from partying.* Laws were meant to be broken. Go ahead, send the cops, these party martyrs would play victim and use Snake's passing as a way to elevate themselves. Play the sympathy card. It was maddening.

As Preacher made his way to the two club officials, he noticed an elderly couple holding each other against the wall in the hallway. They were as out of place as Ron Paul at a Socialist rally. They looked frail and frightened. James smiled at them as he passed by.

Spaniard surprised Preacher with a hug. "Pretty messed up, huh, Nine?" he said.

"What? This crowd or what happened to Snake?" James answered recklessly.

Spaniard gave him a knowing smile. "Both," he said.

"Anyone know who *they* are?" James asked, nodding toward the old couple against the wall.

"Snake's parents," Spaniard answered nonchalantly.

"His parents? His parents are against the freaking wall while a dozen patches are taking up the chairs in the waiting room?" James barked.

"What's your problem?" Magic asked with a growl.

"Bro, it ain't right. This ain't the way we did things. Where's the honor here, we're … you're better than that; this club has more class than that," he said and turned and slowly approached Mr. and Mrs. Vandermere.

"My name is James Walters. I am Richard's friend and pastor," he said with an outstretched hand.

Mr. Vandermere reached for his hand, "Mike Vandermere, nice to meet you. This is my wife, Sylvia."

Holding her frail hand in his, James said, "I am honored to meet you and honored to be his friend. I'm sorry we had to meet like this, but sometimes it's how God works," he added.

"If you say so," Mike said.

"His friends are not very nice," Sylvia spoke softly. "Well, I mean except for you," she blushed.

"Thank you. Well, I can't speak for everyone, many of these guys know Sn —Richard very well and care about him very much.

"I think they're here because he's the president of these clowns," Mike said.

"Mike, please, not now," Sylvia begged.

"Sir, you may have a point. I was with his club for over ten years; there *are* some clowns! I got to know your son very well. He is a good man, a dear friend to me, and he's a great leader of men," James said.

"Were with them; you're not part of this circus now? How did you manage to escape?" Mike asked.

James was starting to see how Snake became so tough, but he liked Mike's delivery and fearless attitude. He figured the man was terrified of watching his son die and that makes brave men out of normal guys. Anger is the by-product of fear every time. James said, "I'll tell you all about it if you'll let me take you downstairs for some fine cafeteria dining or I know a place down the street that makes a great burrito. I'd be honored if you'd join me. I have some funny stories about Sn — Richard you might enjoy," he offered.

"Well, we could use a snack. We just flew in from Philly three hours ago and you know the airlines don't feed you anymore," Mike grumbled. "But we don't want to leave our son's side."

After talking with the nurse, who assured them she would find them downstairs if anything changed, Mike and Sylvia followed James out the door.

***

James charmed the lady into allowing the three of them access to the recently closed cafeteria after assuring her that soft drinks and the pre-made wrapped sandwiches would suffice. "One notch better than non-existent airline food," James joked to Mike and Sylvia.

"Anything will do at this point," Sylvia said. They took their 'meals' to a corner of the room, which would be unhindered by the closing of the main area. They ate in relative silence, pausing only to share nervous smiles. James was swimming upstream; his flesh would rather be working on a motorcycle while listening to the latest Joe Bonamassa CD than being in this uncomfortable position, but he knew the Lord had arranged this meeting.

After some small talk about life in Philadelphia and Mike's thirty years as a plumber, the conversation turned right into the path of an oncoming spiritual train. Mike wondered aloud about Richard's eternal destination in light of being an outlaw biker and all of the bad things in which he'd participated. Surely the 'man upstairs' would weigh all of the good things he'd done against the bad, leaving the heaven and hell scale balance precariously hanging. James took a sip of his coffee and took a deep breath and asked the Lord for the right words for this one.

"Mike, with all due respect, can I tell you what the Bible says about that?" James asked.

"Oh, we go to church; I know all about the Bible and God's judgment," Mike answered.

"Mike, let me ask you something. If you were looking at a plumbing job and the owner of the house started telling you how to do your job because he'd seen a video on 'do it yourself' plumbing repairs, what would you tell him?" James laughed good-naturedly with the question.

"I'd ask him why he called a plumber if he knew it all," Mike said.

James looked at him and then at Sylvia and said, "Let *me* tell you what the Bible has to say about salvation."

Mike smiled and shook his head. Sylvia said, "You have to listen to him now," and laughed.

"Okay, Preacher, do your stuff, but don't take all night."

James laughed and said, "Oh, don't worry, I specialize in triage ministry; it's in your face fast and furious," he laughed. James prefaced his preaching with the guarantee that this was all from the Bible, this was not his opinion, everyone has opinions about everything; the only opinion he was interested in was God's.

"Sin entered the world through Adam. All have sinned and fallen short of the glory of God. The wages of sin is death. Obviously not physical death, because Adam went on to live over 900 years. It's spiritual death that occurred. The chasm between God and man was caused by sin. The Bible prophesied well over three hundred times about the coming of Jesus Christ as the Messiah. He arrived and lived a perfect sinless life, something no man was capable of doing. The law required perfection; we are unable to live in perfection. God's standard is perfection, not ninety-nine percent, not 'good enough,' not close not anything but his holiness. The standard is holiness.

"The Bible says that our righteousness is like filthy rags, which means that on our best day, we suck!"

Mike spit his lemonade through his nose and Sylvia laughed so loud that she covered her mouth and looked around nervously, and then laughed some more.

"I've never heard a preacher talk like that," Mike laughed.

"I'm on a roll, don't interrupt," James smiled.

"God had to send himself as the perfect sacrifice for sin; there was no other way to satisfy his standard of perfect holiness. If you think about it for more than a couple of seconds, it makes perfect sense, even to imperfect man. Enter Jesus Christ! God in the flesh. He went to the cross to satisfy the Father's holiness criteria. If there were any other way, He would have certainly opted out. The cross was a horrible death, but He did it out of a love for us that is incomprehensible. You have to just accept this, there is no way to explain it other than when Jesus said perfect love casts out fear, and that there is no greater love than a man laying down his life for his friends. He spelled it out for us." James paused and reached for his water glass. Additional coffee might be a bad idea as it was nearing ten p.m.

"This is why it is so important for us to grasp what the Lord said to Nicodemas when he said we must be born again. It's a spiritual rebirth; it means that God, through His Holy Spirit, now lives in us. He came to die for our sins, the sin of the world as John the Baptist said, so He could satisfy the 'wages of sin is death' part. He paid a debt that was not His to pay; that is grace. He gave His life *for* us that He could give His life *to* us and live His life *through* us!" James paused as his audience was now wide-eyed. "The sin issue was settled at the cross. Jesus said the only sin attributable to man was that of unbelief. If we fail to believe and trust Him for what He did, that's it, we're cooked. It's not about sin, it's about life.

"We are dead spiritually without His life in us. Forgiveness of sins is not salvation. Accepting the free gift of His resurrected life is salvation and once that has been done, there is no turning back. We are to rest in His work and quit striving to meet a standard that cannot be satisfied aside from Christ's work on the cross and His resurrection.

"Ask Him into your heart and yield your life to Him and watch the most incredible transformation. It's the great exchange! A dead life for eternal resurrected life. Quite a deal, I would say."

"That was quite a presentation there, Preacher," Mike said.

"Beautiful; it really was," Sylvia added.

"Praise God, He took a dirtball biker and softened him up and made him a preacher," James said. "Let me tell you something else. Your son came to my church the first couple of times out of respect for me, but he's been to many services beyond that and he's becoming a regular at my upstairs pool table after church. He is drawn to the things of God. I've been praying for him quite a bit. For all we know, God is speaking to him as we sit here.

"Something's going on up there, that's for sure. We can't control any of it, but we can sure as heck trust God in all of this."

"He's lucky to have a friend like you," Mike said. Sylvia nodded in agreement.

"It's been my pleasure and honor, trust me on that. Richard, you know we call him Snake, right?" he asked.

"Oh my yes, we know that, although we don't know how that all came about," Sylvia said.

"Oh, I can tell you that," James laughed. "Back a dozen or so years ago, the DMC had a run out to Phoenix to our Arizona — their Arizona chapter. Guys were sitting around a fire eating some burgers, the sun was just going down, and a snake appeared behind one of the newest Arizona patch holders. Well, Richard took his knife — you know that crazy big knife he carries," they nodded and smiled. "Well, he took the knife and snapped it from the tip of the blade and it cut that snake in half. You couldn't have scripted it better for a movie and if you didn't get it in one take, you'd never see it again. It was amazing; the knife went a good ten feet and just cut that thing in half." James laughed with Snake's parents. "They were gonna call him 'Blade,' but that name was taken already, so they went with 'Snake,' and boy did it stick. Legendary!"

James said. "Oh man, there's lots of stories. He was —
is — a great guy, a really strong leader and now I can
see where he got all of his good character traits. You
two did a great job with him; I love the guy," James
said to the beaming parents.

"Pray with me, if you wouldn't mind," James said.
He took their hands and they bowed their heads.
"Heavenly Father, thank you for the opportunity to
meet new friends and share your love. Allow us to take
our belief to a new level here, Lord; let us ask you into
our hearts, Lord Jesus; fill us with your spirit, guide our
lives, and give us your resurrected life that we may
know you, not just about you. We thank you that you
took our sins away; now we ask you to live through us."
James paused. "We know you can heal Richard, if it's
your will, Father; please give us more time with him.
Whatever your will, we accept it as your perfect plan.
In the precious name of Jesus the risen Christ, we ask
this. Amen."

Mike and Sylvia held his hands for a few quiet
seconds before letting go with an "Amen," of their own.
James felt that peace again; he knew that he had kept an

appointment that was ordained by God. That was always a good feeling.

An hour and fifteen minutes after they had left the mayhem upstairs, they had become friends and had prayed together. Time flew by as it usually did when James was speaking of what Jesus had done for mankind. It was his favorite subject.

James gave Mike and Sylvia his phone number and insisted they call for any reason. They decided to return upstairs and tell the doctors to go ahead with taking their son off life support. They were at peace that all had been done that could be done. They hugged and agreed to contact him if they needed anything. They would stay for a couple more days to arrange the funeral, thinking they'd make it simple and small, but James told them to be prepared for a circus from the DMC.

It was always a show of respect for a club to honor a leader and James expected at least a couple of thousand people to show. James saw the worry in Mike's face. "Don't worry about anything; the DMC will take care of every detail, including the cost. It's the one thing they actually do right," he said with a laugh.

"Well, we can't argue with them; we just want to spend some time alone with Richard tonight," Sylvia said.

"As you should," James said. "May God bless you both. I'm so happy to have met you," he added.

"Thank you for all you've done here. Keep preaching, son; it's obviously God's will for your life," Mike said with wet eyes.

James hugged them again and walked out the door.

***

He was exhausted. He routinely stayed up until 3 a.m. on Saturday nights. It was only 11:15 and he was completely spent. He figured the hospital had spiked the coffee with that horrible decaf stuff, which in his opinion was not of God. He sat on his bike for several minutes looking up at the clear night sky. The stars were putting on quite a show with their brilliant twinkling against the black space. His phone vibrated and he smiled as he saw Linda's name on the screen.

"Hi honey," he answered.

"Hey you, how's it going?" she asked.

"It's been quite a night. I met Snake's parents and had a sandwich with them. They're nice people; they're hurting but I got to minister to them," he said. "It was a real blessing."

"Well, everything here went fine after you left. I just wanted you to know I was home safe and all is well at the church. The Prophets are amazing, James; are they always like this? I mean I couldn't raise a finger. Someone was always there to help me; it was amazing. Then they had someone walk me to my car. Thank you; I know you had that arranged," she said.

"I'm glad they took care of you, and no I didn't arrange anything. I wish I could take credit for that; it's just how they, how *we* roll," James voice cracked.

"Honey?" she asked, "you okay?"

"They're going to pull the plug on Snake, babe. I'm trippin' on that right now. I was so sure that God was doing something here, I don't know ..." his voice tailed off.

"Hey, you're in the right place; Snake's parents needed you tonight. You know this is bigger than it looks right now; hang in there honey," she said.

"I know, thanks for that; I appreciate you more than you know. I'm gonna ride back to the building, I'm crazy tired for some reason; I'll call you tomorrow. Sweet dreams; I love you, babe."

"You, too; get some sleep. I'll make you a big breakfast if you come see me in the morning," she offered.

"You gotta deal. Goodnight, hon."

CHAPTER NINE

A few Prophets were hanging out in the parking lot when James got back to the warehouse/church/bikeshop he called home. This living arrangement was no doubt some type of zoning violation but so far no issues with the city or county. Even with the success of the shop and the outrageous growth of *Real Church,* he saw no pressing need to add rent to his list of payables. He and Linda planned to marry in six months and her house was the perfect base for the happy couple to begin their journey together. She lived in a quaint area of Redlands, just minutes from the craziness of San Bernardino; it was the perfect set up.

"What are you guys doing here?" James asked his Prophet brothers.

"We stay till the preacher is home safe," laughed Carl. He was at least forty-five minutes from his home in Anaheim. This was indicative of how this club differed from the last. Brothers extended themselves and as the Bible says, considered it their reasonable service.

"Go home!" James yelled. "I appreciate you watching over everything, but it's past your bedtime, little brother," he said with a smile.

"How's Snake doing?" Carl asked.

"Not good, bro; they're pulling the plug. I still can't get my head around this one," James answered.

"We'll keep praying, brother. Hey, service was awesome tonight, bro; it's off the hook. There are more people here every week; you're gonna need a bigger building!" Carl's enthusiasm was duly noted and appreciated by the preacher.

"Dude, I was going to hit the swap meet tomorrow, but I'm never going to make it. Can you pick some stuff up for me if I text you what I need?" James asked.

"Sure, bro, no worries; hit me up and I'll find you whatever you need." James jotted down a few items on a scrap of paper, handed it to Carl with three one hundred dollar bills, and told him to shop carefully. He hugged the other two brothers and they prayed for safe travel (traveling mercies) and one more time for Snake — just in case God didn't hear the other fifty prayers.

James watched as the Prophets roared off into the night. It was a cool night; he hadn't noticed earlier. It felt good. He planned to sleep late, at least till eight, and then roll to Linda's for the breakfast she promised.

He entered the big dark building, lit with only a couple of warehouse lights, and struggled to reach the front lobby. As his eyes adjusted to the gray darkness, he stopped and began to cry. He fell to his knees in his new church and felt the oppression of the enemy weighing heavily on his spirit. He hadn't cried this bitterly since Michelle died. It was physically exhausting and he was already on the verge of collapse. The enemy knows when to strike. James knew all the verses about resisting the devil such as, "greater is He who is in me than he who is in the world." Nothing helped. He was crushed, devastated by the pending death of his friend.

And someone had tried to kill him that morning, too; what the heck was going on? A horrible thought — *If this is what I get for serving you, I don't know if it's worth it* — hit him. With that thought, he regained his strength and cursed out loud. "No way are you going to beat me, devil; I know what you're trying to do!" he yelled. "My Lord is Jesus Christ. He is my rock and my fortress. You need to deal with Him if you want any part of me," he continued. "I know who I am and I know whose I am; my identity is in Christ now. You have no power here; you have no hold on me anymore!"

As he stood up and began to shake off the attack, his phone buzzed in his pocket. *Jeez, what now?* he asked before he looked at the phone. It was Magic. *What the heck could he want?*

"Nine? Dude, you better get back over here right now. Do you hear me, you freak? You preacher freak, get over here now!"

"Magic?" Nothing. *What's the world record for hang-ups in one day?*

His phone buzzed again. This time it was Snake's parents.

"James, this is Mike. I'm sorry to call you this late but something is happening over here. Richard's vitals have improved, and not just some … I mean they are extremely good. We were going to sign the papers, James; we almost made a huge mistake! We were going to sign them tonight, here, now; can you come back? I'm afraid something is going to reverse or something; this is amazing." Mike's voice reflected a roller coaster of emotions.

"I'm on my way, Mike, praise God; whatever is going on, praise God!" James hung up and jogged to his bike. "Lord, whatever you're doing, I'm not tired anymore!" He thought to call Linda but decided to wait until he knew something more concrete than … "Get over here now!"

Strangely, he made every light on the way to the hospital. Seriously! There were no fewer than eight stoplights between his church and the hospital and every one of them was either green or turning green. He couldn't remember that happening before. It was a surreal ride. Fast, too. No guard to worry about at this hour. He ran up the driveway, careful to avoid that one nasty speed bump, and parked next to the four Harleys at the hospital entrance. He recognized Magic's right off and parked his next to it. Magic was as good a sergeant-at-arms as James had ever seen. The fact that he'd been there the whole time spoke volumes. No doubt the only time he didn't roll with Snake was from home to work. *A convenient time for this 'accident,'* James thought. The list of people who would know this information was very short. This was an attack from within, he was sure of it.

The elevator ride was painfully slow, the door was slow to open, everything in the place was slow. James was all jacked up after the phone calls and the fast ride and now ... patience. The silence of the elevator was interrupted as the door opened to a small but excited crowd spilling out of the waiting room. He saw Mike and Magic laughing ... together. Sylvia was close to Mike, but leaning against the wall with her eyes closed and a smile on her face. Cedar and several patch holders were inside the waiting room, expressionless.

Magic was the first to see James.

"Preacher man! Dude, I don't know what you did in there, but something happened. Snake's numbers are getting better by the minute, bro!"

"I didn't do …"

"James, Oh James, God bless you." Sylvia rushed to him and grabbed his face with both hands, something his mother would have done years ago.

"Great job, Preacher," Mike added with a slap on the back.

"You guys, this is great but I didn't do anything. All glory to God; this is — what are the doctors saying?"

"That's the best part, bro; they're running around like someone switched patients on them," Magic laughed. "They are freaking out; it's great," he continued.

"Honey, they said that with the vitals where they are now, the only remaining question is what kind of damage has been done; he could either stay in a coma indefinitely or come out of it any minute," Sylvia said.

"In other words, they don't have a clue," Mike added.

"Can we see him?" James asked.

"Sure, I mean I think so; they let us see him about twenty minutes ago," Mike said.

"Would you mind if Magic and I went in for a minute?" James asked.

"Have at it; you're the reason he's still with us," Mike insisted.

"Mike, God is the reason. I know this seems like I'm splitting hairs, but please give God the glory. He's in this in a mighty way," James said.

"Fine; thank you God," Mike laughed.

James smiled and shook his head. "Let's go, bro," he nodded to Magic.

"After you, Preacher man," Magic put his huge arm around his friend's shoulder and led him to the room.

***

Nothing much had changed. The sounds were the same, still eerily quiet except for the beeps and clicks. The oxygen mask was hanging from his chin; evidently the breathing tube had been removed and he was breathing on his own. It was shallow but rhythmic, not labored. James wished that someone would change the bandage on his head as the blackened blood stains would be tough on Mike and Sylvia. Maybe it was his imagination but James thought Snake seemed to have better color than the gray tint exhibited earlier. His lips were moist; James wondered how that was possible. Every time *he* was in the hospital he had to bribe people to put those dang ice chips in his mouth. 'Dry mouth' was on the list of things he hated about hospitals. There was a long list.

Magic told Preacher to take the only chair in the room and he moved toward Snake. His big hand trembled as he attempted to hold Snake's hand. James laughed to himself, quite sure Magic hadn't held a man's hand in quite some time, if ever. He could not imagine this guy was ever a small child dependent upon his parents. Maybe he crawled out from under a rock.

Magic looked at his old friend. "What's so funny?"

James looked at him with big eyes and said, "Nothing, bro; I'm just happy."

Magic turned back to Snake. "Hey Snake, quit screwin' around, bro. You got our attention, you can come back now," he urged. "Nine Ball, I mean Preacher is here with me, bro; we're hoping you come back soon cuz I don't like ridin' with this guy. Bro, it don't look right," Magic laughed as he looked at James and flipped him off.

James reached for his phone and sent a quick text to Linda, letting her know that he was back at the hospital and told her briefly to keep praying because things were changing around there. After he sent the text he stood up and walked over to the other side of the bed and took Snake's other hand.

"Heavenly Father, we thank you that you answer prayer, we thank you that your healing hand is upon our brother, we ask Lord that you continue to breathe life into our brother Snake. Baffle these doctors with your power and might, Father. In Jesus' name we ask this, amen."

"Amen," said Magic.

"Hey Nine … I mean Preacher, what does Amen mean?"

"It means agree — we agree with God on His plan and will. We can ask all day but it's got to be in accordance with His will, so we blather on about what we want and then at the end of it all we agree with God as to His plan."

"Oh, well, Amen for sure then," Magic said innocently.

"Amen indeed," James said.

"Kinda makes you think, huh Nine … I mean Preacher. Dang, bro, sorry I keep calling you Nine but you've always been Nine Ball to me, bro," Magic said. This was the first time James had ever seen any semblance of humanity from Magic. He wasn't about to waste the opportunity.

"Oh yeah, I think about this stuff all the time. You remember back when Tucson was killed at the party? I mean that kicked my butt for a while, but dude, and I know you're tired of this God stuff from me, but Snake will tell you, there was a heavy spiritual scene right before he died, bro; God, dude, He was *so* there that night, it was nuts."

"Yeah bro, Snake was blown away by what happened out there. He kept telling me that I wouldn't have believed it. He said that when I checked him on lettin' you out like he did, bro, that was unprecedented stuff you pulled."

"You're tellin me? I was messed up bad on that deal. It may have looked like an easy walk but I felt like the rope in a giant tug of war. I knew what I had to do. There was no question about that, but you guys were … are my brothers; we've been through everything together. Even knowing what I had to do, it was still the hardest thing I ever did," James said.

"I guess I never thought of it from your standpoint," Magic said.

"Selfish punk," James said, then they both laughed out loud.

"Can you guys shut up? I'm trying to rest."

James and Magic looked at each other in utter amazement, then at Snake, who was smiling with his eyes still closed.

"Are you freaking kidding me?" Magic said to no one in particular.

"Snake?" James asked hesitantly.

Snake spoke slowly and deliberately. "I could ... use some ... water if you guys are ... done reminiscing."

"Sure, bro, I think. I'll ask the nurse if it's okay; they'll want to know that you woke up and are ready to go home," Magic laughed.

"Dude, your mom and dad are outside. Can I bring them in?" James asked.

"In a minute, bro. Don't go far tonight; you and me, we gotta talk. Something crazy is going on here, bro. I had some weird dreams." Snake's voice faded.

"Rest, bro; I'll be here," James said. What he didn't say but would have if Snake would have heard him was that his weird dreams were probably the result of the guard rail smashing his head in. He'd reserve judgment until he heard what they were about.

CHAPTER TEN

Morning came and with it the worst headache James could remember having. He had rolled home at 2 a.m. after sitting in Snake's room nodding off again and again. Snake didn't wake up again; he was obviously done talking for the night but he was alive and God was awesome. The best part was telling Snake's parents that he was awake and joking and that meant he was going to be alright. He was lucid, if only for a minute.

James determined to hit the gym before Linda loaded up the calories. He'd been training regularly and if it weren't for his graying temples and facial hair, he could physically pass for a man twenty years his junior. Old age could not be stopped, but it could be disguised somewhat. He had created a workout that lasted at most thirty minutes and kicked his butt in the process. No longer could he spend two hours a day banging weights; his body wouldn't allow it. He found that this new abbreviated version worked well enough.

Riding his new bike after a workout and a shower was the perfect cap to the morning. The chill against his still-damp hair was invigorating and by the time he arrived at Linda's place, he was positively giddy. The thought that Snake had improved, the time spent with Snake's parents, his beautiful fiancée, his dodge with death, and the resulting new Harley had him feeling pretty good. Sure, someone had tried to kill him, but that would work itself out in due time. No use dwelling on things he couldn't change. God was still in control and the peace which that affords cannot be overstated.

Linda stood at the doorway wearing an orange and yellow sundress and holding a steaming cup of black coffee. James stopped on the walkway and marveled at her beauty. Her strawberry hair was held behind her ear by an orange flower and the morning sun was dancing off the delicate gold necklace he had bought her for Christmas. "Wow, you're stunning. I love that dress, babe; you're pretty darn hot!" he gave her a big smile.

"You're not so bad yourself, honey; that T-shirt isn't nearly as wrinkled as yesterday's," she teased.

"Nothing but the best for you, baby girl," he joked back and added, "I *did* shower."

"Well then, come on in."

After a healthy breakfast of cage-free eggs, organic milk, and butter on whole grain toast James joked that he'd better hit up the In & Out for lunch to balance things out. Linda made a face and shook her head. Sometimes he just said things to drive her crazy. They talked about Snake and his parents and about how great it was the night before with Magic. James told her that they were in the middle of a great work of God and things might get even crazier. He wasn't trying to scare her off — he loved her much more than he wanted to — but he felt he needed to prepare her as much as possible for the impending spiritual warfare. Linda was no coward; her new-found love for the Lord had kindled a desire to serve Him in a mighty way and being a pastor's wife was a blessing that she would embrace. He knew that as a married man, he'd put her interests ahead of his own but still behind God's. *He* had to be number one. James was sure he could prioritize.

The danger that James continued to face would have to be dealt with. He would need to get to the bottom of the attempt on his life; that business must be finished before he could have a wife. He would never knowingly drag her into danger, even if it meant losing her. He would trust God on this, though easier said than done, as his flesh was already hatching plan after plan for payback. He must not yield to those temptations. God's way would be the only way. This might well be the biggest challenge in his almost four years of walking with the Lord. Easier to counsel other people on how to live than to put it into practice in one's own life. Physician, heal thyself.

***

There must have been twenty bikes out front. The cops were there, too! He had wondered how long it would take before they were called in. Nothing like a few dozen outlaw bikers to disrupt an otherwise peaceful setting. Two city cruisers and two San Bernardino Sheriff cars. No doubt several more deputies were within a mile of the place. James thought that sometimes the presence of law enforcement actually served to fuel potential problems rather than mitigate. This was true with outlaws who, when left to their own, would usually take care of their business and move on without incident. After all, they were there to visit a fallen brother, not rob the place. There was a fine line, though, when these guys mixed with citizens. Quite incendiary, actually; all it would take would be a couple of cute nurses or a jealous boyfriend and this powder keg could blow. *Here's a travel tip*, James thought: *stay away from outlaws whenever possible; don't pet them, don't feed them, don't talk about how you used to ride, nothing — just keep walking, nod respectfully, and keep walking.*

James resigned himself to one more elevator ride to the fourth floor. Kit had told him to wait to be called before injecting himself into the mix, but after the night before, he thought he'd be able to move freely upstairs, especially with Magic around. He knew that he'd need to lay back and wait for Magic to engage. It was like a one-night stand: one person falls in love and runs headlong to the other the following day; invariably there is tension. *Really, it's like that?* Great analogy, bro. Not. James didn't want to wager on how Magic would welcome him today with all those big, bad, ugly DMC hanging around.

***

"Preacher man! What took you; you been sitting at the pool all morning?" Magic said with a big laugh. The Preacher tentatively exited the elevator waiting for the other shoe to drop. Nothing.

"Yeah, you know, having half a grapefruit and some organic eggs on the patio; sorry I'm late," he answered. If they only knew how true that was. He was laughing on the inside. "How's he doing?" James asked.

"The same, but that's a good thing according to the doctors. They are still trippin' over what happened last night. I heard one of them say that in twenty years he'd never seen anyone come back from that kind of brain injury. It's really got them scratching their heads," Magic said.

"Good, God is good. The prayer was to confound the doctors that God would be glorified. That's cool," James said.

"Yeah, his numbers are all good, everything is getting stronger, even his breathing is stronger than when we saw him last night. He looks good, too; good color. He hasn't said a word since you and I saw him. If there wasn't two of us in there, bro, I would be questioning my sanity right now cuz nobody believes me," Magic said.

"You mean all I have to do is deny I heard him talk and you go to the farm?" James asked with a smile.

"You do that and I'll have to settle up when they release me," Magic smiled back.

"*If* they release you," James joked.

As the two men joked with each other two doctors approached them. "Is there a man called Preacher with you gentlemen?" one asked.

"That would be me," James said.

"He asked for you. We thought he was calling for a preacher but he said, 'Preacher, not a preacher.' He was quite clear."

"When did he ask? We thought he was still sleeping or whatever you guys call it," James said.

"No, he woke up briefly, asked for Preacher and drifted off again. If you like, go sit in there and talk to him; it might help," the doctor said.

"You come with me, bro," James said to Magic.

"Nah, bro, he asked for you. Go check it out and then if anything changes, come get me," Magic said.

James searched for any sign of a bad vibe from Magic since Snake had only asked for Preacher, but there was no indication that it bothered him in the least.

He opened the door quietly and entered the room. Someone had opened the blinds so the light of day had filled the place with life. There were several x-rated 'Get Well' cards on the table, several flower arrangements, which made him smile. The 'Downed Biker arrangement' wouldn't be a big seller at Proflowers but you make do with what you have. He could all but hear Snake saying, "Dude, get rid of the flowers," and he made a mental note to see Snake so healthy that he would demand the flowers be taken from the room. It would be a sure sign of returning mental health.

He pulled the lone chair up to the side of the bed and took a seat. He looked at Snake for a couple of minutes and said, "Hey bro, it's Preacher; I hear you're asking for me?"

He waited for a minute and then, hearing no response, said, "Ah, not talkative today, huh? Well, that's cool. I'll just sit here and read to you; how's that?"

Again, quiet. "Fine then." He turned to the book of Hebrews in the New Testament, one of his favorites. He began in Chapter seven and went to eight just reading along to his sleeping friend.

Snake moved his hand and extended an index finger, but since the preacher was not paying attention, Snake said, "What laws?"

James stopped. "What bro?"

"You just said ... I will put my laws ... in their minds; I thought you said that Jesus fulfilled the law. Now you're saying I will put my laws in ... their minds," Snake said with great effort.

James smiled and said, "Praise God, yes! Yes, your brain is still working just fine!" He paused and then continued, "The Law differs from His laws. The Law is the Old Covenant. His laws are the two commandments that Jesus gave us upon which all the others hang: He said to love God with all of your heart, mind, and soul and to love each other as ourselves. You understand that if you love God and love your brother, you'll never find yourself doing any of the other "don'ts." It's impossible to love God with all of your being and go out and commit adultery and rip people off; the two actions are diametrically opposed to each other. Yes, brother, Jesus fulfilled the law, we sure as heck couldn't and God knew that we couldn't, so He sent Jesus. His sinless and righteous life has been imputed to us when we come to Him by faith," James finished.

"Good deal," Snake said, "Thanks for coming, Nine ... Preacher, whoever you are," Snake slowly added.

"Get some rest, bro. We're here for you whenever, whatever," James said.

CHAPTER ELEVEN

Magic looked up from the magazine he was reading as James made his way toward the waiting room. Most of the DMC were cordial now; guess the word was out to behave, at least for now.

"Well?" Magic asked.

"Dude is asking heavy theological questions, bro; he's gonna be fine, "James answered.

"No way; really?" Magic asked.

"True fact, bro; he blew me away in there. He's in and out but when he's in, he's all in," James said.

Outwardly, Magic was happy, which was not normal; the guy was usually a pretty dark cat. Whatever suspicions James had harbored earlier were dismissed by now. Magic had been there through it all and his relief regarding Snake's condition was genuine. Some of the other guys were expressionless throughout the whole ordeal. This represented either disregard or disinterest; James found either unacceptable.

"Thanks for being here, bro. I know it's weird for you, but I appreciate it and I know Snake does, too. You're a class act and if I've been a jerk it's because I miss havin' you around ... sometimes," Magic said.

"I'm down, bro, my prayer is that the rest of the DMC comes to a peaceful place with me and with the Prophets MC," James answered. "I'm going to check on Snake one more time and then I need to get back to the shop; I'm behind on some work over there. I'd like to see you at the church again soon. Maybe you can stay longer next time," James laughed.

"I'll be there when Snake makes it back over there; deal?" Magic asked.

"Deal."

James turned and took two steps toward the room and stopped.

"Hey Magic, this is unrelated and random, but that's how my head works sometimes. I need some paving done out back of the warehouse, not much, just a parking extension. Do you know any asphalt guys?"

"Yeah, one, but you probably don't want him around. It's Cedar; he's the ops manager for a company in Yucaipa ... called Four Seasons Paving," Magic said.

"Well, maybe I'll hit him up. Work is work; it ain't personal to me. Thanks." James continued down the hall to Snake's room and walked in.

"My parents think you're a great guy," Snake said, his eyes still shut.

How did he know it was me, James thought. "I figured them for great character judges," he answered.

"They're old; they're slipping," Snake said.

"You had us worried, bro. Praise the Lord, though; He pulled you out with a healing that these people will be talking about for years to come, lemme tell you," James said.

"I ain't arguing with you any more, Nine ... I mean Preacher," Snake said. "I even heard the "M" word out of one of the nurses this morning. These medical people are pretty cold, dude; you don't talk miracles with them," he continued.

"Well, bro, seeing isn't always believing, even though it should be," James said. "Jesus told the Pharisees the same thing when they kept asking for more signs and miracles. Faith is a gift; the Holy Spirit imparts a measure of faith and we either build it with the Word of God or we let it fade from lack of use," he added.

"I want your faith, bro," Snake said.

"It's a personal relationship with the living Christ. He might just blow you away with the level of faith you achieve," James smiled. "The thing you need to understand, what everyone needs to understand is that it's not the size of your faith that matters, it's the size of your God, the object of your faith. Jesus said many times what a faithless bunch we were and that if we only had faith the size of a mustard seed — those things are really small, by the way — we could move mountains.

"He was basically telling us we have no faith. Always remember that it's God who does the initiating and we the responding, not the other way around, bro. Beware those who keep emphasizing their great faith and what great faith does. It's the object of our faith that has the power, not faith itself. It's a slippery slope, bro, when we start thinking we can make God do whatever we want if our faith is big enough. That's not biblical faith, that's sorcery. That's Satan in the garden of Eden saying, "You can be like God."

Snake just stared at his friend for a minute.

"How did you learn all of this, bro? I watched you go to into prison! You always had a sharp mind, but it was scammin' and dealin' and fixin' stuff, not this heavy theological stuff; it's pretty crazy." Snake continued, "Dude, what the heck am I going to do with who I am and talking about faith and Jesus and stuff; it's a bit of a contradiction." James started to laugh. "It ain't funny, dude; it sucks," Snake said.

"I'm not laughing at you bro; I'm laughing because you and I had this talk about six months ago the night of the party," James said. "You let me out because you were sure that God had called me into ministry and my continuing association with the DMC was incongruent with that plan," James said.

"Incongruent?" Snake asked, "Save the twenty-dollar words for someone else, brother," he laughed.

"I learned it the other day and I've been dying to use it in a sentence," James laughed. "Semantics aside, bro, it probably looked easy from your position, but I was facing the same decision. I'm not saying you need to do anything; let's not get caught up in that trap," James said.

"Let God orchestrate things, bro; just allow Him in. I mean he healed you here, let's not lose sight of that; if He did that He did it for a reason. Let me ask you this, assuming there is a God of the universe and He's all powerful and mighty and loving and there is an eternity, would you do what He asked you to do if you were sure it was Him doing the asking?" James asked.

"Of course," Snake replied quickly.

"Exactly, bro. Now all we need to do is figure out if He's real or imaginary," James said.

"Really Nine? Dude, you and I know He's real; it's ... well, my only problem is ..."

"You are your 'only' problem," James joked.

"True dat. That's what I was going to say before you had to butt in," Snake said. "You're lucky I'm tied to this bed."

"I know; I'm taking my best shots now before you can reach me."

Their conversation was briefly interrupted by two curious doctors who came to check readings of some kind.

"I'm going to start charging you guys, especially when you bring in new doctors to show me off to," Snake said.

"I'll check into the possibility of an insurance rebate of some kind," one doctor said.

"Wow, a doctor with a personality. Nine, check this guy out. Hey, doc this is my pastor; he's the one who caused all the problem with my delayed departure," Snake said.

"Don't blame me; blame God!" James said.

"Well, whatever happened, I've never seen anything like it, not even close, so maybe you guys have something here," the doctor said.

"Oh, you can bet on that, Doc," James said.

After a few more notes were taken, the two left the room with a quick nod of their heads. They were probably happy to escape; these two were scary-looking dudes if you weren't prepared. Snake looked huge even lying down.

"Hey Nine — I mean Preacher; sheesh, I'll never get used to that. How you figure I lost my bike on a curve I've ridden every freaking day for seven years?" Snake asked. "All I remember was that it was a great ride right up until I dove through that guardrail," he added.

"You don't think I've been wondering that same thing, bro? I've already been up there snoopin' around and I found something interesting. Can you think of anyone who would want you gone?"

Snake smiled and said, "Only a couple hundred or so people come to mind."

"Yeah, that's what I thought you were gonna say," James laughed.

"It's not your problem, brother. I appreciate your concern and all but you've got your own club to worry about," Snake said.

"That's a helluva thing for you to say to me," James said, quoting their favorite movie, *Tombstone*. "That would be true if I didn't have a twelve gauge leveled at me yesterday morning. Someone tried to remove me from this planet, blasted the front of my bike, and sent me for a tumble out on the back highway."

Snake was wide-eyed. "Where'd this happen?"

"I was on my normal run up to Big Bear and some punks in an old Chevy pickup shot at me through the back window."

"You gotta be kiddin' me; how are you standing here?" he asked.

"Long story, bro. Suffice it to say it's another of those 'God things' that keep happening around us," James said.

"Where's your bike?" Snake asked.

"In a pile behind the Harley dealer. It's gonna be a total loss so I took the liberty of buying a new Glide, same color, like nothing happened," James said with a smile. "Knucklehead set me up pretty good; I had to come up with a couple grand and he got me approved. I'll throw whatever money the insurance company kicks down at the balance and should have it clear within the year," James said. "You know I hate bike payments."

"Me, too. I guess I'll have to see what they do about mine," Snake said.

James looked at his friend. They both knew that the DMC would have his bike better than new in a few days; they had the connections and the resources to make that happen. James did miss that part of the outlaw life, but caught himself as he realized that his resources were infinitely larger.

"So they blasted you clean off your bike and you're walking around unhurt and ridin' a new Glide a day later?" Snake asked.

"Same day, brother. I had that new Glide on the street just a few hours after they shot me."

Snake was laughing. "I love it. That'll drive them crazy, bro; whoever it is, they gotta be freaking out." James just smiled.

They stopped talking while the nurse checked Snake's numbers once again.

"You're quite the talk of the hospital," she said to Snake.

"I'm here all week, baby; two shows a night. Nobody does two shows anymore," he laughed.

As the door closed behind her Snake spoke quietly, "You said something about finding something interesting at the crash site. What's your conspiracy theory, Nine Ball Preacher man?"

James took a second to formulate his answer. "I saw a patch of oil on the street. It's a perfect square and it was exactly where it needed to be for your long turn to become street surfing. It just seemed weird to me, the square pattern, not like someone just dumped oil. I'm willing to bet that your front tire has that oil on it and you never stood a chance. You know that highway like the back of your hand, bro; no doubt you hit that lean at fifty-plus and all it took was a little oil to wreck your night. If someone wanted to "off" you, that would be the place. You go headlong into the guardrail and those posts are freaking six-by-sixes. If you miss the guardrail you fly seven hundred feet straight down before you bounce off the first rock. You should have been another wreath on the side of the road."

It was Snake's turn to think before speaking. "You tell anyone about your findings?" Snake asked.

"Yeah, I called the cops and the newspapers. And I put it on Facebook," James said.

Snake closed his eyes and smiled as he slowly shook his head.

"I miss you too, bro," James said.

"You have any ideas on who mistook you for a duck?" Snake said, changing the subject.

"Maybe, but not anything I can prove ... yet."

"It's a little weird the both of us going down at almost the same time. Guess it was our turn," Snake said.

"Maybe, but I think we both had some help. We sure had some help from the Lord or we wouldn't be here. But we should keep our … my theories between us for now. I need to head out now and check some stuff out, but I'll get back to you soon; that is, if I can get to you now that you've attained rock star status."

"Be careful out there, bro. If they want you dead, they're gonna keep trying till they get it right," Snake said.

James smiled. "All those years as an outlaw and nobody shot at me. I join a Christian club and now I'm public enemy number one. Go figure. Oh, and I saw how you used the doctor interruption to change the subject back there; you're still pretty slick even with a dented head. We will continue this later, my brother, over the pool table."

CHAPTER TWELVE

"That bike was yanked outta here yesterday, dude," the voice bellowed from behind the half-closed door. James figured they would have already come by and grabbed Snake's bike, but it was worth a try.

"Pretty messed up, was it?" James asked.

"I've seen worse," came the voice. "There was a lot of damage to the right side, pipes were ground off, and the front wheel was bent, probably from the guard rail post, but the frame seemed okay. Needs a new tank and fenders, but it can all be fixed." The voice finally had a face as the kid walked out from the office. "I hear the guy got messed up pretty bad. That sucks; you know him?"

"Yeah, I know him, he's a brother," James answered. He was fighting the old habit of judging as this guy was not impressing him with his mannerisms; he was avoiding eye contact and that drove James nuts. His dad taught him to look a man in the eye, shake his hand, and introduce himself with his full name.

"You DMC?" the kid asked.

"No. You go to church anywhere?" James asked.

The kid stopped and looked up. "Church? What's that got to do with anything?"

James tossed his card on the counter. "There's a great church over off of Tippecanoe. Saturday nights ... you should come by," he said and then turned and walked out the door.

***

Harley dealers are all closed on Mondays. It takes some getting used to if you're looking for parts after a long weekend of riding, but corporate figures this is the only way to ensure a day off for their employees. If it were up the customers, these poor folks would be on call 24/7. It has fostered some decent after-market parts and accessories businesses and James regularly defaulted to one in particular off-the-beaten-path in Yucaipa near Beaumont, another fifteen minutes or so to the east. It's a nice, straight, fast ride on a bike, but a boring trip in a cage of any kind. Well, any kind that *he* had access to; no doubt it's a fun trip in a six series BMW.

James was out looking to purchase a ride stabilizer for his new bike. After some jokes and catchin' up, James had what he came for and was about to leave when Chet, the sixty-plus ex-something or other outlaw from Florida made mention of Cedar and the DMC. James stopped and slowly walked back.

"Yeah, how is Cedar doin'? He workin on Snake's bike by any chance?" James asked.

"Yeah, he called earlier and wanted new front and rear wheels, some nice billet aluminum ones. Said he wanted two tires, too."

James wondered about the tires as Snake was nuts about having good rubber at all times. He remembered several occasions where other brothers would use Snake's "used" tires for months before needing new ones.

"Hey, if you could get Cedar to bring in the old tires, I'd probably buy them from you, Chet. You know Snake's tires are usually good for a few more miles; they won't fit my bike but I could use them at the shop.

"No problem, bro; I'll call you if I can get them. What about the wheels, you want a shot at those, too, if they're not bent or anything?"

"Yeah, sure; lemme know what they look like," James said. "Oh, no need to tell Cedar that I'm wantin' those tires; just keep that between you and me."

"Sure thing, Nine. Good to see you again; you'll love that stabilizer, bro."

James smiled. "I can't wait. See ya next time, Chet; thanks again."

CHAPTER THIRTEEN

There were three messages on the shop answering machine. James hadn't gone completely digital. He gave his cell number to club members and other friends, never customers. They could call the shop. One call was from a neighborhood pizza joint with some special deal, one call was a new customer — James would call him back right away, and the last call was from Jerry, whose son ended up in prison after he'd killed James's very dear friends in a drunken crash, just days after James had been released from prison himself. For some crazy reason known only to God, James had become a regular visitor to Rudy at Chino Men's Prison. The two had forged an unusual friendship under some of the strangest circumstances imaginable. It was this weird relationship that proved to James that God was capable of anything. The Bible says with God, all things are possible. James believed it, Rudy was starting to believe it, and Jerry had actually visited the Saturday night service a few times, though not in the last three weeks. James never asked why; maybe a better pastor would care more. Whatever.

James scheduled some work with the newest customer who had been referred by Magic of all people, and then sat down and punched in Jerry's number. After an awkward attempt on Jerry's part to explain his lack of church attendance, he got to the point of the call. Rudy was being transferred to Corcoran for the remainder of his twelve-year sentence. James knew the kid would be out in half that time, but the official book on this punk was twelve years.

The preacher first put his friend at ease by telling him that he wasn't missed at church and if he wanted to screw off on Saturday nights it was no skin off his ... well, suffice it to say that James straight told him that he didn't care if he went to his church or not, just that he attended somewhere. Second, he agreed to visit Rudy in the next couple of days and for sure before he was transferred upstate.

Jerry was just trying to remain sane while his son was doing time. Like any parent in this situation, he was just going through the motions until the release date and then would probably spend his time worrying when his idiot kid was going to do something insanely stupid again and land back in the joint.

Truth be told, it would be easier in many cases if the kid were dead. You don't worry much about a dead guy, but the living ones could make you crazy. That was the preacher's best advice on prison and kids. Best not to have him counsel just anyone; he could be a bit abrupt. His best success was with these knuckleheads *before* they got to prison. His Tuesday nights had become the youth ministry nights or as the preacher referred to them, 'The Teenage Drama Hour.' There were rave reviews thus far and the kids were bringing friends, so maybe his approach wasn't quite as bad as several parents had noted.

Linda had fielded several such complaints from distraught parents and she'd done a praiseworthy job of deflecting concern. Her biggest challenge was to intervene before, God forbid, the parents reached the preacher. He'd already told one father to take his sniveling wife and hit the road and come back when they had a clue.

Linda was the only person who could approach the preacher about his methodology and she was careful with her timing. James was a man of God and had a big heart but he was adamant about his not being a "pastor." He was a preacher. He definitely had the gift of communication and a great ability to teach, but he could be a bit impatient with those who didn't catch on quickly or readily accept his New Covenant message of forgiveness.

Basically, he was a street fighting outlaw biker with rage issues from way back. God was doing a work in his life like many around him and James knew from what pit of hell he was rescued. He was grateful and joyful, if not happy all the time. He'd been quoted as saying, "Sorry if I don't run around like a happy idiot all the time," when questioned about his darker periods. He noted that the great theologian Charles Spurgeon was depressed much of the time, too, so maybe with the blessing of being called to preach, he was a bigger target to the enemy and depression was a chink in his armor.

He struggled every day with thoughts of old addictions and although he 'had a handle on it,' as he said, the temptation was disturbingly strong at times. James was training himself to recognize these spiritual attacks and thus far had defeated them before a foothold was gained. He reasoned that the enemy would love to get him loaded and fighting again, which would lead to the destruction of his relationship with Linda and ultimately the church. The responsibility was growing larger every day; he would need to remain wary of the tactics of this very formidable enemy.

He noted that the Apostle Paul referred to Satan as a worthy adversary. James could relate to that terminology. He noted during many counseling sessions that such an adversary was never knocked out in the early rounds of a fight; instead, those types tended to stick around for a fifteen-round split decision. A very dangerous foe.

Then there were the accusations whispered by the enemy. "Who are you kidding? You're an outlaw, not a preacher; you're a dirt bag, this woman will never stay with you; your business won't last, nothing will last, give up, go back, get loaded, have some fun." This stuff came at him late at night as he woke violently from terrible dreams. It was almost like the devil hung out in his room and waited for him to wake from the satanic theater that flooded his mind. The cold-blooded fear that gripped him in the dark of night was paralyzing in its reality, like a power pressing him against his mattress. As he scrambled to remember tactical scripture, the lies came at him in relentless torrents, confusing his every effort to combat the assaults.

These dreams were commonplace as a child but had diminished in their frequency and intensity by his late twenties. Now they were back and with them, a mature and educated production quality designed to terrify a mature and educated man. In short, the cinematography was much improved and the plots too heinous to discuss in the light of day with civilized people. Consequently, they stayed where they did as a child. Inside. James yearned to trust the Lord to intervene but his deepest fear was that the dreams would continue and his faith would waver as a result. It was better not to ask, just in case. This fear, the lack of trust — which was inevitably a lack of faith — would serve the enemy's purposes. Steal his joy and sow the seed of doubt. If this outlaw was going to serve God publicly and throw a wrench in the works, at least he would be dark and miserable in the process.

CHAPTER FOURTEEN

"Vampires are pussies," James told a defiant Rudy through the prison intercom. The kid looked slightly more rested than the last visit a few weeks ago, but still malnourished and terminally tired. He fit right in. Only a true sociopath could eat and sleep and function normally in prison. Evidently Rudy had opted to read the latest fictional swill about the undead and their ability to foster romance with the living. "Jeez, dude, I left you with some pretty good books on reality and you opt for this crap? How old are you?"

"Hey, lighten up, man; at least it got me thinking of something outside of this dump for a few hours, " Rudy said.

"Do yourself a favor, bro, when you go up north, don't let these guys see you reading romance novels, even if some of the characters are dead," James chuckled.

"I hear ya," Rudy said.

The preacher surveyed his surroundings; several young women were visiting their worthless boyfriends and husbands. A couple of them even showed up with small children. Great place to raise a family. He reflected on how he did his three years well after his wife had died of cancer. It was the perfect time to do some time, if that made any sense at all. What he meant by that was if he was going to go to prison for a three-year stint at some point in his life, it might as well have been after she was gone. He had little tolerance for married gangsters or outlaws, and he regularly preached to the teens not to drag anyone else into your stupidity. The outlaw life did not include a white picket fence and two-point-five kids.

He shook his head with a Tourrette-like twitch and refocused on Rudy.

"So, aside from fantasizing about pale half-dead chicks, what you been doing with your time, Rudy?"

"Dude, please, I'm not *that* into the books; I just read one. Everything else is the same in here. I don't need to tell you … you know. You heard I'm being transferred to Corcoran?" Rudy asked.

"Yeah, your Pops told me. Guess it could be worse, bro; at least it's not Pelican Bay or Folsom. It's just a place Rudy; it's not forever." James looked at the kid and fought the urge to feel sorry for him. Rudy did kill his friends, so he should be glad the kid was squirming a bit about the transfer. Sometimes this God thing could really cut into your revenge enjoyment.

"You think much about what we talked about last time?" James asked, changing the subject.

"Yeah, some," Rudy said.

"You have any more brilliant insights about the non-existence of a hard-to-miss God?" James asked with a smile.

"I don't want to pretend about this, dude. I could just tell you, yeah you're right, I believe, everything will be fine, see ya later. I can't fake this just to make you happy," Rudy said.

"Don't worry about me, bro, I don't care either way. I'm just layin' this on you; you gotta deal with your unbelief, not me." James said and then continued, "My job is to present the gospel of Jesus Christ to you, to answer your stupid questions, and then it's between you and God."

Rudy shook his head and said, "You see how you are, man? If I don't go along with your plan, I'm stupid."

"Awww, Rudy, I'm not saying you're stupid — God is," he smiled.

"What are you talking about now?" Rudy asked, visibly irritated.

"Psalm 14:1 says the fool says in his heart, there is no God," James answered. "It's like we talked about last time. You don't want a God in your life because you don't want accountability, but it looks like you're being held accountable anyway, unless you just volunteered to be here."

"It's not like I didn't listen. What you had to say made sense, but I just go back and forth with it; it's like a struggle," Rudy said.

"Yeah, well, that's a good thing, bro; it means that God thinks you're worth saving. There is an epic struggle in the heavenly realm for your soul. The devil wants you and he's a tough customer; he's the best liar in the history of ... well, the history of everything. The Bible calls him the father of lies, so watch yourself. I'll keep praying that the scales fall from your eyes and you can see the truth shining like a beacon."

Rudy stared at his teacher and said, "Don't you ever have doubt?"

"No, I don't have doubt — well, not anything that lasts — but I do get assaulted on a regular basis by the enemy. Like I said, he's a tough customer and when he lost me, he lost a shot caller, an influencer, a first stringer and he don't like to lose, so he keeps coming at me. I mean like right when I least expect it, I get hit with some crazy thinking, some really bad thoughts, heavy accusations about who am I trying to fool and stuff like that. That's temptation, spiritual warfare — not doubt. Big difference. I know what time it is, bro; Jesus is the risen Christ and the enemy's attacks only serve to strengthen my trust and knowledge in my savior."

Rudy was nodding his head. "Yeah, I get that. It's kinda like those old commercials with the angel guy on one shoulder and the devil on the other and they're tuggin' at some dude to do somethin' or not do somethin'," he said.

Just then James had a thought. "Rudy, you ever hear the story about the two wolves?" he asked.

"No, what's that all about?"

"My dad told me when I was very young — I just remembered it — about an old Indian and his grandson. The old guy tells the kid that all men have two wolves living and fighting inside of us. One is evil and full of pride and jealousy and greed and malice and all sorts of bad stuff and the other wolf is good; he's full of love and forgiveness and humility and kindness and generosity and stuff like that. The little kid asks his grandfather who wins, and the old man says, "The one you feed."

Rudy looked at the preacher and said, "Looking at you, you're obviously the grandfather."

"Looking at you, you're lucky there's an inch of glass between us," James smiled. He promised to stay in touch with Rudy through regular mail, letters and whatever he thought to send. Rudy promised to read whatever he sent.

"Remember what I said: you won't do the whole sentence, you can rebuild and make something of your life. Your sins, though many, were forgiven at the cross but you need to access the life of Christ through faith and trust, not just belief. The devil believes and it ain't doin' him any good. Turn from your unbelief; trust me on this." He tapped the phone against the glass before hanging up. Rudy tapped his and nodded his head to his strange visitor. Then he watched him walk out the door.

CHAPTER FIFTEEN

Tuesdays are the busiest days of the week at Inland Performance Systems. One day removed from the weekly Harley dealers' day off and everyone is trying to get their bikes done before the weekend. James loved living upstairs from his shop as it allowed him an early start time so much of his work could be completed before his first mechanic showed up at eight-thirty. He had completed one job and had lined up the week's work for his crew. If nobody got crazy, everything could be finished up by close of business Friday. That would mean any new business would have to be pushed to the following week and with any luck he could sneak away a couple of days and do some fishing or maybe take an overnight ride somewhere. Being the owner had some advantages, as long as things were running smoothly. The guys got along pretty well … for bike mechanics.

Justin was the senior guy, who started at eight-thirty every day like clockwork. He was the guy who knew the location of every tool in the shop and God help you if you didn't put it back in the right place. Travis, on the other hand, would show up between nine and eleven every morning but would always work an honest day regardless of how late that kept him in the shop. He kept to himself and always worked with his iPod wired to his ear. James liked him; he was a bit off on a social level but there wasn't a bike he couldn't figure out, which drove Justin crazy.

That being said, one p.m. was a busy time for the cops to show up. As his office overlooked the parking lot, James saw them coming long before the downstairs crew was startled by their entrance. He was halfway down the stairs when he yelled into the shop. "Can I help you gentlemen?"

"Are you James Walters, aka Nine Ball?"

"Not anymore. What do you want? No offense but you guys are bad for business."

"Just a couple of questions about your accident last Saturday," one cop said.

By now, James had made it all the way downstairs and was face-to-face with his visitors. "Ain't nothin to talk about. My front tire blew out and I folded up the bike and praise God, I walked away with a couple of scratches," James said.

"That's amazing; how fast were you going when it happened?"

"Why, you gonna write me a ticket?" James smiled.

"Not this time; just wondered. You're pretty lucky," said the shorter cop.

"I guess about fifty; that's the last thing I remember before I went down."

The taller of the two was looking right into his eyes when he said, "One of our guys was over at the dealer getting his bike checked out. He overheard the parts manager talking about how your bike looked like it had shot imbedded in the fairing and the front tire, like maybe your accident was caused by a shotgun blast."

"Well, that would have certainly caused my front tire to blow out," James said without expression.

"Yeah, it certainly would have, are you leaving out anything from your story here?" he asked.

"Not that I can remember; it all happened pretty fast."

"Seems a bit strange that a new front tire would just blow out like that," the tall one said.

"Yeah, but I got a new bike out of the deal so what the heck, right boys? No harm done," James said.

"You afraid your pretty girlfriend's gonna find out someone took a shot at you?"

"Fiancée. I'll make sure you boys know where she's registered so you can send a nice gift. I like pretty girls. You guys still don't ask, don't tell?" he asked.

"That's the military, smart guy," the short one snapped.

"Oh, my bad," said James.

The entire conversation took place in the vestibule. James never invited the deputies any farther inside. He fought the urge to ask them if they wanted any coffee, still a bit wary of law enforcement.

"Nice shop; pretty big. Is this all yours?" the short one asked.

"You guys are either new around here, dumb, or messing with me for some reason, so which is it?" James asked and then before they said anything he added, "You know I'm out of the DMC, you know I have a church here on Saturday nights, and you know about my shop, and if you don't know all of this then I don't feel safe with you guys on patrol. What is it you want from me? I'm busy and like I said before, my customers see five-o out front and they go elsewhere."

"Take it easy there, pastor, you're a bit jumpy for a man of God, aren't you?" the tall guy asked. James just stared at him.

The deputy continued, "I was at the Badlands that day you tore that place up. I remember who you really are … Nine Ball."

Looking at his partner, he continued. "You should have seen the damage this guy did; it was pretty impressive, I will admit that. What was it — two or three guys you put in the hospital that day?"

There had to be a reason for this visit aside from his being blasted off of his bike. These guys didn't care if another outlaw got shot or stabbed; he understood the score here. What bothered him was his inability to figure out their angle, and he had always prided himself on outsmarting these guys.

The tall deputy broke the silence with, "Seems mighty strange that you and Snake went down in the same week, hell, same forty-eight hour period for that matter. I guess you two aren't as bulletproof as you thought."

James smiled, "We had a long run at the table, dude. I guess the old saying is true: it's not *if* you go down, it's *when*. I appreciate your concern."

"Yeah, well, if you think of anything you might have forgotten, you know like maybe you were in shock or something, give us a call." The lead deputy handed him his county business card.

James glanced at the name — Palmer — and then stuffed it into his shirt pocket; he knew *he* would never use that card, not for any reason. He might, however, pass it on in the interest of justice and his civic duty. "Snake's accident might be more interesting to investigate than mine. That is, if you're really interested in solving crimes," he said.

Short cop, obviously feeling inferior to Palmer, jumped in. "You saying that his crash wasn't an accident? Maybe someone tried to bump him off?"

"Bump him off? You watch too many old movies, buddy. I'm just saying if you were real investigators there's more to see up there than down here. I'm fine; Snake's in intensive care."

"If you know something, you'd be smart to talk to us —"

"I'm not doing your job for you. There's something wrong with that crash; figure it out or move on. I've got work to do and your cars out front are scaring people away. Thanks for stopping by; if you want to come to church, it's seven o'clock every Saturday night. Drive different cars, though; you guys have like family Crown Vics or something?" James said.

Palmer laughed at that comment. "Okay, Nine Ball, we're outta here for now; see you in church."

***

"… the heck did those guys want?" Justin asked.

"Asking questions about my accident, buggin' me, same ol' stuff," said James.

"It's never good when those guys learn your address," Justin said.

"Address? They know what I had for breakfast, bro. I guarantee they watch this place all the time; they don't believe that anything good can come out of here. They don't have a clue what's really going on. They hassle my Prophet brothers all the time, always jammin' them up with questions. They're in a time warp; that's why they're ineffective, always reacting ... and slowly at that. Maybe they'll come to church and learn something."

"You invited them to church?" Travis piped in.

"I didn't think you could hear anything with that thing in your ear!" Justin said.

"I hear more than you think."

"No disrespect, Preacher, but why did you …"

"I asked them for two reasons: one, I'm a Preacher and I care about their eternal souls and two, I don't think they'll come!"

They all laughed at that.

"Covering your bases, eh?" Justin said.

"Sort of."

"You're a better man than I am," Justin laughed.

"Well, duh!" said James.

CHAPTER SIXTEEN

James reached across the table to avoid the second ring as the phone was still in 'shop' mode. "Yeah."

"Nine, it's Chet. I can salvage the tires and you're right, they're in great shape. The rear wheel is perfect but the front wheel is bent to hell; what you want me to do?"

"I'll be by in the morning. I'll take the rear wheel and the tires, but can you work with me, bro? I'm running out of money taking my fiancée to these fancy restaurants," James said, giving Linda a wink.

"Always, bro; see you tomorrow. Bring me a breakfast burrito from El Cap and we'll work it out. I'll clean them up for —"

"No! Don't clean them! Sorry, bro, didn't mean to freak you out, but if it's all the same to you, can you leave them just like they are? I have my reasons."

"Yeah sure, bro, no worries; they'll be nice and dirty when you get here."

Linda grabbed his phone and stuck it in her purse.

"You said no phones," she pouted.

"I lied. You better turn off the ringer if you're gonna keep it in there. You'll look foolish trying to dig it out of there while it's ringing off the hook at the bottom of that thing," he said.

"What's that all about … don't clean what?" she asked.

"That was Chet out in Yucaipa. He's got some parts from Snake's bike that I want to buy — tires and a wheel. I think someone tried to kill Snake by spreading some oil on the highway up there and I want to take a good look at the tires to see if there's any residue on them." He looked straight into her eyes.

"You're serious?" she asked.

"Very. You know I said all along that something wasn't right about the whole crash story," he continued.

"Yes, but where did this oil theory come from?" she asked.

"I rode up there and took a look around and spotted a distinct square pattern of some kind of oil on the highway right in his path. I have no doubt that he hit that spot on a curve and slid into the guardrail. It should have killed him either from the impact or flying off the hill."

Linda looked at her future husband with raised eyebrows. "Honey, you're scaring me. What ... why would someone do that?"

In the five seconds it took him to answer, he saw all that was beautiful and pure about her. She couldn't fathom this kind of violent insanity; it had no place in her civilized world. She was right. She was also in love with a guy to whom this was normal and expected. He was going to drag her into a lifestyle that accepted crazy as normal, where the police were never called and where problems were solved quickly and where straight answers were not always forthcoming, all under the guise of protection. What was he doing to her? Deceit could have no place in this relationship. If she couldn't handle his lifestyle and he was unwilling to change, then she had the right to make an informed decision about her future.

"I honestly don't know, baby. Snake's the president of a nationally recognized outlaw motorcycle club. That position carries with it some inherent danger. We ... I mean *he* will figure this out; it's not his first rodeo. The Lord has brought him through this for a reason; he's cool with that and is doing well. He even asked a few faith questions. I'm encouraged," James said, desperately hoping to change the subject of the conversation.

"Well, I'm glad you're out of *that* club. At least you're safer with the Prophets ... I think. They ride around too fast, too, but at least nobody is trying to kill them." Linda said. "Oh, I almost forgot, I started painting the large spare bedroom. I figured that you'll need an office at home when we get married. I know you like your quiet time before service and I thought it would make a nice 'man cave'-slash-office. I'm using a medium tan with an accent wall in ox blood. It will look rich, like a law office or something. I can't wait to show you."

James was amazed at her gear shift from the Prophets to room painting, but decided to let it pass. He tried to sound thrilled, though he was sure it fell a bit flat. "Wow, that's sweet of you, thank you," he said, thinking that she was trying to pull him away from his church office. He was a creature of habit and it had been awhile since he was in a relationship; he was squirming in his seat. He laughed to himself: *you wanted to change the subject smart guy; well she changed it*. Now he'd rather talk about attempted murder … it was easier.

"Pick your battles," his dad used to tell him. What he meant was that some things were just not worth the trouble. Some cans of worms should be left unopened. He had a few months to work out the details of a home office versus a church office. He might acquiesce to the pre-game office ritual but there was no way he would tap out on the after-service 'upper room' gatherings. His big quandary was whether to tell her the whole truth about his own brush with death. He would rather face Magic in an alley than tell Linda that someone took careful aim and blasted him from his motorcycle, *Easy Rider* style.

"What are you thinking about, James?" she asked.

"Me? Oh, nothing, just trying to picture ox blood all over the walls." He smiled. He had her; she smiled and shook her head.

"Don't play dumb biker with me, mister; I know you pretty well. You aren't going to get many more miles with that act with me."

"Speaking of miles, you want to take a ride with me to Big Bear on Saturday?"

"That's your quiet time; are you sure you want me to be there distracting you?"

"Who said anything about distracting me? You can't just sit there and be quiet for three hours?"

Linda was so pretty, even when she pretended to be mad. James was falling in love. And he liked it. "I'll think about it; we have a couple of days. You're 'mister spur-of-the-moment' so I'll just wait before I give you an answer," she said.

"Fine with me, baby girl; you know I roll early so if you're going, be there by eight. I will always be ready for you."

"That's sweet ... I think," she said.

CHAPTER SEVENTEEN

The tire on the workbench looked like a scene from a recent episode of CSI. James had the high intensity gooseneck light bent over the sliced rubber pieces with his needle-nose pliers sufficing for tweezers. There was evidence of some oil on a portion of the front tire, which Doctor Preacher and his eight-inch straight knife had cut into manageable pieces. Next to him stood Gordon Richie, a chemistry professor at UC Riverside, who also attended Real Church on Saturday nights almost without fail.

Since James was not prone to asking law enforcement's opinion on anything, he had floated the idea of a possible favor with the good professor on Saturday, who agreed to help any way he could. James figured a mild-mannered professor with a theory backed up by laboratory findings might accidently communicate such findings to the appropriate authorities.

If politics produces strange bedfellows, then amateur crime forensics might be a close second. A six-foot tall biker with shoulder length hair and tattoos over muscle contrasted Gordon's five-foot six-inch classic endomorphic pear shape. Regardless, these two were on a mission and Gordon was of the opinion that if they were going to secure a sample from the road, they had better hurry. The properties of the substance would be easy to ascertain but if water and other dilution took place, it might prove difficult, especially if the goal was to prove something beyond a reasonable doubt at some future hearing.

They agreed that Gordon would take the tire and its evidence back to the university and the preacher would roll up the hill and swab a couple of samples, bag and tag them, and act as courier to the lab. It was early afternoon so the men agreed to meet at five p.m. at the university and then to dinner in downtown Riverside at the restaurant of Gordon's choosing.

***

James let Kit's call go to voicemail as the reception half way up the mountain was spotty at best. He knew he was in a bad spot so decided to call his friend and 'P' when he got to the bottom of the hill.

It had been well over a year since the crash that took Marc and Robin, and James found himself going days and weeks without thinking of them. Not today. Maybe it was the forced solitude of a mountain ride or maybe he was just due for a dose of melancholy. He never felt it coming; it had a tendency to overtake him at the most inopportune moments, but today was a good day for some reflection. For a change he wasn't scrambling around town like a lunatic. He had intended to spend some quality time with the Lord on this run up the hill to gather his share of the forensic sampling; however, his mind had other ideas.

Almost from the moment he rolled out of his driveway, his mind was laser locked on thoughts of his friends and why they had to die, why couldn't they have enjoyed Real Church at least for a year. He caught himself entering the realm of self pity, guilty perhaps of ingratitude and not willing to accept God's will entirely. We can't pick and choose; we either trust Him with everything or we trust Him for nothing. To be used by God, to avail oneself to God, one has to trust Him completely.

God's richest blessings are reserved for those who exhibit faith, not just belief. Remember, without faith, it is impossible to please God. We have to have faith that His will and His timing are perfect. The reason they were taken when they were was God's business with them and no amount of James' leaning on his own understanding of how things should have gone played into God's decision. As He said in the book of Job, "Where were you when I made the world?"

The enemy is a crafty dude; any distraction is a good distraction. He had masterfully robbed James of almost an hour. Sixty minutes that were intended for quiet time with God became a distraction over the past and no amount of yearning could change what had occurred. He chided himself for falling for this elementary attempt at diversion. *Check and mate*, James smiled with a thought that could only come from the Holy Spirit. This week's sermon would be on the danger of distractions. There were plenty of scripture references to putting God first. There was "Seek first the kingdom of God and His righteousness and all these things will be added to you." There was "Lean not on your own understanding but in all your ways acknowledge Him and He will direct thy paths." Oh yeah, "God has not given us a spirit of fear but a sound mind," and other stuff like that which illustrates God's desires that we keep our priorities and He will take care of everything. "Delight yourself in the Lord and He will give you the desires of your heart." Oh, this would be fun.

James had often thought of himself as a spiritual guinea pig where all manner of craziness manifested weekly and he had to make some biblical sense of it all by Saturday night! It was an awesome responsibility and great fun at times. Like now, where he could feel the power of the Lord taking what the enemy meant for harm and turning it into something wonderful for his two hundred hungry sheep. He would gladly lead these people in the things of God, regardless of the warfare that was often aimed at him.

It dawned on him that the highest honor he could pay his two dead friends was to evangelize the lost and teach the gospel of grace until the Lord called him home where he could accept an eternal assignment and see his friends again.

***

"Yo, Kit, what up, bro? I missed your call a while ago, I was riding up toward Crestline and had no signal," Preacher said.

"No problem," came the gruff voice. "Me and Tio are heading to the stateline early tomorrow to meet some guys who might want to come our way, maybe start a Vegas chapter …"

"Really, Vegas, huh?"

"Maybe!" Kit barked. "Don't tell anyone, it's not for sure; we just thought you might want to get the break-in miles on your bike all at once, if you're not busy."

"Nothing that my guys can't handle at the shop. Just get me back before Saturday night at seven," James laughed.

"Don't start; we're not going all the way to Vegas. These guys are meeting us not quite halfway, but we like to ride so it's no big deal. You in?"

"Yeah, we can meet at the shop if you want and just roll up the 215. I'll have coffee ready; maybe I can figure out how to work the toaster and we can eat something."

"Cool, we'll see you at your shop at 5:45. God bless you, bro," and he was gone.

James marveled at both Kit and Tio, as they seemed not to need sleep like normal people. Like himself, for example; nothing like a good night's sleep which, as he pondered his meeting in an hour with Gordon, then dinner, then who knows what else, he wouldn't be getting as much as he planned. Friday mornings were his 'sleep in' days, but not this week.

CHAPTER EIGHTEEN

Dinner with Gordon was nowhere near as unpleasant as he thought it would be. Just goes to show you that if you just reach out to people, they often reach back. James wasn't anti-social, but he had days where it's best to avoid him. He was introspective at times and came off downright mean. He'd catch himself, recently more than ever, and apologize even if it meant calling someone a day later and copping to his rude behavior.

Gordon surprised him with his relatively conservative viewpoint, which James thought rather rare for a college professor. He was no William F. Buckley, but he held his own. That was quite refreshing. They both agreed that to effect society, the grace of Christ must be preached. James was excited to speak to someone who felt as he did that no amount of local political involvement would affect the national stage, but if millions of people came to the saving knowledge of Jesus Christ and let the spirit of God live through them, the country would regain its sanity.

Gordon agreed to call James when his testing was finished. The plan, primitive as it was, involved

Gordon's presentation of the evidence, what Preacher called 'gift wrapped' to the authorities with a theory that would involve a late night visit to Four Seasons Paving company. James wasn't above trespassing if it would solidify their conspiracy theory. Once proven internally, it would withstand proper investigative techniques. He just wanted to make sure; no use getting all crazy if his idea was all wet. In a nutshell, he had pegged Cedar as the middleman; he was too stupid to be a shot caller. That individual or group remained unidentified for now.

Snake was the big target. James was shot because he hurt Cedar's pride and the quick but sloppy retaliatory plan to blast him off his bike was hatched and carried out before anyone could put the brakes to it for its stupidity. Had it been successful, nobody outside of the DMC nucleus at the hospital would have figured Cedar for the hit and although Preacher was a former Doomsayer officer, the urgency to solve the crime would be low. 'Former' being the operative word.

Because of Preacher's inability to resist rubbing it in Cedar's face, he figured the idiot for another whack at him and if he had Cedar's temperament pegged, it would not be long before the next attempt. The guy had no class. Any respectable outlaw would wait until the target was no longer the least bit wary; he'd known guys who waited years to exact vengeance, but James didn't count Cedar among the more intelligent characters in the mix. He was a reactionary, another reason he couldn't be the shot-caller behind any of the Snake business. However, his connection to a paving company with an oiler that most likely matched the one used to coat Snake's path made him perfect for the grunt portion of the caper.

CHAPTER NINETEEN

The lazyboy chair, donated by Prophet 'Doc,' proved a most comfortable seat in which to study and write the outline for the outline of each Saturday's service. Yes, James outlined the outline. His upstairs office was becoming quite the retreat. It was nearing ten p.m. and he decided to read a bit before a visit to the paving company at around 2:30 a.m. All he needed was a small sample from the sprayer of the oiler truck that he theorized would match the substance gathered from the crash site and Snake's front tire. He hoped that the yard's front gate security cameras would provide time stamps of the truck's departure and arrival on the night of the crash. James would have to thwart those cameras tonight and hoped that the black clothing and face mask would ensure his stealthy maneuvers in the event they captured the image of an intruder. He was betting against detection at all, but at the very worst, he would not be identified. He certainly would rather not tip his hand before the county could do its job; less chance for tapes to disappear, etc.

A rather involved Charles Spurgeon treatise, coupled with the cushiony headrest, had James fading in and out of consciousness. *This chair is ridiculously comfortable*, he thought. A weird sound caused him to look up and notice his phone vibrating on the coffee table. He sat up to see who was calling at this hour. The phone screen indicated *unknown caller*. "Preacher here," he said.

"Your girlfriend smells really nice," the raspy voice said before the phone went dead.

Dread filled him. A feeling of terror stunned him as he fumbled to locate Linda's number. He hit the button and prayed out loud, "Please Lord, please let her be okay; she's so innocent, please ..."

"Hi, it's Linda; you know what to do at the beep."

"Babe, jeez, please be there," he said in panic. Should he keep trying the phone? Should he blast over there on his bike? He grabbed his cut and his helmet and ran to his bike. "Dear God, please," there was no peace now, no scriptural comfort forthcoming; he was out of his mind with fear. His mind raced through horrible possibilities, though he tried desperately to block the horror, the fear; he was frantic and he was on a motorcycle. He rode like a madman, ran two lights, redlined every gear and almost lost control twice before the freeway. *Calm down, God's in control, you can't wreck it, you've got to get there*, he thought as he rode.

Linda's street was dark and her porch light was on, which made sense to James as he locked up his brakes and slid to a stop. With a practiced down stroke, the kickstand was in place and he was over the seat and running to the wide-open front doors ... both the security door and his freshly-varnished-birthday-present-antique-wood door.

James ran inside, yelling her name through the lighted long hallway as he headed toward her bedroom, which, too, was lighted. "Linda!" he screamed. "Honey ... Linda!" Everything was quiet but for his breathing as he waited for her response. He ran through her bedroom and the master bathroom; her robe was on the bed. What the hell was going on here? He ran back out to the hallway and stopped in pure fright. It looked like thick red ... blood flowing from under the door of the spare bedroom.

He punched the door open, overcome with relief as the light from the hallway revealed the overturned ox blood paint can, the contents of which crept across the floor and over the threshold. James hit the light switch and saw an empty room, save for the rolled-up plastic drop cloth. He turned to walk out when he heard the muffled sobs. His eyes went to the drop cloth and he took two steps and dove to his fiancée's bloody body wrapped in the film. "Oh Jesus, no!" he screamed as he tore the plastic exposing her bruised and punished body. Blood was pulsing from countless wounds.

Linda whimpered as James lifted her to hold her to him; he brushed her hair from her bloody face. She felt so cold. She had been stabbed so many times that her blood filled the folds of the plastic. James fumbled with his phone to dial 9-1-1. He leaned to her and said, "My God, baby, who did this to you?"

"You did," she said as the blood flowed from her mouth.

"9-1-1, what's your emergency?"

***

James abruptly sat up in the chair, his neck was soaked with sweat. It was 10:45 p.m. The nightmare drove him to his knees and he sobbed uncontrollably. The enemy had invaded his peaceful surroundings once again and this time with an arsenal of condemnation. Who was this poser, this 'preacher' who would put his woman in harm's way without her knowledge? What kind of man endangers his fiancée? *Who are you fooling with your phony church and your half-in half-out pseudo commitment to the Prophets? You're an outlaw and you belong back with the DMC; you're not a preacher!*

"Hello?" Linda answered on the second ring.

"Hi … oh man, it's good to hear your voice. Are you alright?" he asked.

"Of course; why wouldn't I be? What's going on, honey? I think the question is, are you alright?"

"Yeah, I am now. I was reading and must have dozed off and man, did I have a nightmare. I love you, Linda; you know that, right?" he said.

"Yeahhhh, I do. I love you, too, baby," she said.

"Okay, well, sweet dreams. I'll see you tomorrow. Sorry to be so weird, but the dream was not good," he said.

"Well, regardless, it's nice to get an 'I love you' call before bed," she laughed.

CHAPTER TWENTY

Preacher changed his mind; he was going to the paving company at midnight. It made no sense to wait until later; it was an in-and-out job, nothing he hadn't done a dozen times before. He couldn't stay in that room another minute; that nightmare was horribly real and he needed to shake it from his mind.

He wasn't really stealing anything, just a little trespassing. The plan, after a quick survey of the place a couple of days before, involved climbing a fence and landing on a fifty-five gallon drum that was conveniently located below.

The exit would be the tough part, as the distance was about four feet farther to fall. At fifty-one, he regularly visited the gym, so he was sure he could still climb a lousy seven-foot tall cyclone fence. He had a folded tarp that would buffer the barbed wire and his leather chaps and jacket would provide further protection against the intrusive metal.

There was an easier way, but that would take another half a day and James wanted Gordon to be able to pick up the specimen first thing in the morning while he was rolling toward the state line with his brothers.

He was right; entrance to the yard was a breeze. He landed perfectly on top of the barrel and hopped down without a sound. A quick jog to the oiler and the sample was obtained and bagged within sixty seconds. James was feeling pretty happy with himself as he jogged back to the barrel. How his earlier reconnaissance failed to identify the reddish brown Doberman became problematic as the dog's incessant barking only began when he was about five feet from his leap. For the second time in several days, thick leather chaps saved this aging biker from disaster. He was able to shake the athletic dog and levitate over the seven-foot fence in a display of agility usually reserved for a much younger man!

His landing was reminiscent of his exit from a bull back in Chino twenty years earlier. Thankfully, a small patch of grass greeted him upon re-entry to the earth. That hamstring was taking a beating lately. James grabbed the tarp and made sure his sample was intact as he ran ... well ... jogged the half block to his bike.

Minutes later he was laughing down the freeway back to the safety of the upper room. This was his first taste of outlaw adventure in years and it felt good. It would have been a great time for a few beers, but he settled on a half of a half of a five-milligram melatonin and a bottle of ice cold Perrier. Morning would come early. He labeled the sample and left it in a manila envelope addressed to Gordon and placed it on the seat of the motorcycle, which Justin would see first thing. He notified Siri to wake him at 5:30. He didn't like her very much.

CHAPTER TWENTY-ONE

Thoughts of Linda invaded his brain the second he registered the wakeup call and his location on the planet. Melatonin kicks his butt, however, the need to secure as much sleep as possible was of paramount importance. With only fifteen minutes before the boys would arrive, James crawled from bed and took a shower. These guys were maddeningly prompt so the clock was ticking. He employed the coffee maker and the machination of reducing the coffee cherries to powder began. The aroma was already filling the room, and with some timing, the hot nectar would await his exit from the shower.

No sooner had James filled the third cup than he heard the bikes. He chuckled, his earlier estimate confirmed. He could set his watch to the Prophets MC. If they said 5:45, they meant it.

"Morning, Sunshine." Tio's smile was a welcome sight. He was disarmingly charming at times, though this only served to lull his unwitting victims into believing he was harmless. He was capable of almost constant mental and emotional abuse, all the while strengthening his brethren and helping to develop a sense of awareness. It was all in good fun, but as James was learning, a Prophet had better develop a thick skin around this sentry.

Tio continued, "rocket fuel ready?"

"Just poured you a thick batch, bro; there's lemon bites in the bowl," Preacher offered, referring to the sinfully sweet bite-size lemon cakes that had become a favorite among the inner circle after Saturday service and a staple at the monthly club meetings. Tio's face lit up as he headed straight to the rust-colored plastic bowl. Kit's unmistakable laugh indicated his awareness of the aforementioned lemon cakes.

"Life's short," Kit exclaimed.

"Eat dessert first," they all said in unison. It was the unwritten code of the Prophets MC. They did like to eat.

The preacher had never been one to enjoy meals. Oh, he loved the food; it was the company and conversation that this loner had avoided much of his life. He was beginning to learn the value of fellowship in its pure form and he was finding that meals shared with friends were opportunities to foster intimacy, another foreign concept to this maladjusted outlaw preacher. Linda was helping him accept the fact that his schedule was not etched in stone, nor was it arrogantly more important than that of others. James was coming to grips with his impatience. Albeit slowly.

"You gassed up, bro?" Kit asked.

"Yeah, topped her off last night," James answered, smiling to himself as he fueled right before his visit to the asphalt company.

"Let's roll then," Tio said.

James double-checked that the envelope was resting on the bike at Justin's bay. He was comforted to know that Gordon would be finishing up the crime lab duties later that morning. James hit Linda with a quick, "Rolling with the Prophets this morning. Call you later. Can't wait to see you. Luff you," text and locked the front door, hit the automatic rear door button, and rolled the bike past the threshold, entering the security code at the rear of the building. He fired his bike and quickly caught up with the two club leaders as they arrived at their bikes that were parked out front.

"Me and Tio up front; you'll never keep up with that factory fresh cruiser, bro," Kit laughed.

"Yeah, we'll see what happens when I get to five hundred miles, bro. I've only got about two-twenty left and I'll see what she'll do," James answered. He knew he'd never keep up with Kit's bike but at least after break-in, it would be somewhat close. One thing he knew he never wanted to do was ride these things too hard the first five hundred miles. He cautiously ran between sixty-five and eighty-five, being careful to run the bike at set rpms for a few minutes before adjusting speeds. It seated the rings more uniformly. It was not as crucial as it was with the older models but the break-in was still a ceremonial requirement if nothing else.

***

As the cold morning air hit them, James was once again thankful for his windshield. Tio had a similar bike, but Kit liked his Dyna model with lots of wind in his face. The preacher admired his leader's old-school attitude but deep down enjoyed the measure of warmth that the windshield provided. *You really are getting old*, he thought.

True to form the two front runners blew him away entering the 215 North. Riding through San Bernardino required a good deal of concentration as the freeway, though recently renovated, possessed some strangely engineered curves that appeared as random interruptions in an otherwise enjoyable ride. Once the road straightened out north of town the two leaders let up a bit so the preacher could catch up. James was inwardly struggling with his pride; up until his prison term and subsequent repentant conversion from a heathen outlaw to a born-again Christian, he'd served as the Road Captain to the Doomsayers MC. Although it was almost five years since, he still remembered leading packs of fifty-plus bikes on high speed and lengthy rides all over the west coast.

To be relegated to bringing up the rear of a pack of three was tough on his ego, good for his spirit, but tough on the flesh. That was the point. These guys were always 'checking' each other and every club member to ensure the humility learned as a prospect would never be too far removed. Every one of us fights the battle between spirit and flesh daily; it's nice to have such devoted friends to keep a guy from getting too full of himself. James needed it more than most.

The church was growing and he was reaching rock-star status on Saturday nights. James needed his spiritual beat-down every week to remind him that it was God who was blessing Real Church every day, not the preacher.

The three rode up the Cajon Pass, which is a wild ride as the elevation ascends from near sea level in San Bernardino to four thousand feet at the top in just a couple of dozen miles. It's a fun ride up and a crazy ride down. The imminent sunrise was turning the eastern sky a gorgeous violet and purple as it began its ten-minute Technicolor transition from dark to light. Using nothing but head nods and smiles, the men shared the morning's majesty between them at eighty miles an hour.

These encounters bond men's souls. If these many moments are shared often and long enough, brotherhood is forged. It's something that cannot occur in a car, or 'cage' as bikers refer to their four-wheeled counterparts. Every moment, every road condition, obstacle, hindrance, or detour further cements the bond. Weather, near misses, blowouts, and breakdowns all contribute to the weave of the fabric of a biker's life with his brothers.

Kit was visibly agitated that the strawberry milkshakes advertised via billboards for miles before Baker, California were not available at 6:45 a.m.

"Like there's a bad time a day for a milkshake," he said with disgust.

"Let's hit them on the way back, " Tio suggested.

"Yeah, I'll still want one then," Kit allowed.

"Let's take the opportunity to top off the tanks here, boys," Tio said.

"Yeah, I'm under half a tank already," Kit said with a big laugh. He loved to burn gas at a high rate; it meant they were rolling fast. He often said, "If you want good gas mileage, buy a moped."

James knew firsthand how the outlaw world rolled and these Christians took a back seat to nobody once the kickstands were up. They rode like madmen. He smiled.

The meeting was planned for 9 a.m. in one of the cafeterias at Cactus Kate's, a casino that had grown from a roadside joke thirty years ago to a high-rise detour from the busy streets of Las Vegas. A favorite stop for truckers and travelers, its bright lights lured motorists for one more try on the way out of town or a warm-up for those heading to sin city. James laughed as he imagined the many shortened Vegas trips as unsuspecting gamblers headed off at Cactus Kate's, never to recover. He knew all too well the trap of the casino. Years ago, before his spiritual U-turn, James was what his own father called a 'Suicidal Gambler.' Dice, craps, the devil's bones, his only game. He could travel through a casino with nary a stop at blackjack or poker, he laughed at the terrible odds of the mechanical and computerized games, but the seduction of a boisterous craps game, well, that was quite another story.

James was a student of the game, knew all the odds, the sucker bets and the advantages of each the player and the house. Rational and disciplined at this table, alcohol his only nemesis, he rode some of the most manic rises and falls imaginable. His wife called it 'Mr. Toad's wild ride' every time he stepped to the craps table. As he walked the floor, he wondered if he could handle the call of the dice and wondered how he'd play sober.

CHAPTER TWENTY-TWO

Casinos all sound the same. The incessant bells and ringing, the din of voices, and the occasional exuberant screams from the frequent but random payoffs throughout the room invite the casual visitor to join the fun. The veteran players ignore it all. This is more a pitting of the wills, the respectful salute before battle. The casino loathes but courts this player. He can do damage but everyone, even the player, knows that the final advantage belongs to the house. As the song says, 'you gotta know when to hold 'em and know when to fold 'em.' There must be a pathology behind the desire to get the upper hand in the game you're not supposed to win.

Everyone loves the long shot and the underdog. The trick is to know your moorings before you belly up to the table. If you're there to get rich in one night, you are fuel to the machine. If you're willing to match wits with the devil with savvy and poise and an earmarked stake, you can take a piece of him once in awhile.

With Tio and Kit in the meeting, James was free to wander for an hour or so. As a patch holder, he was expected to gracefully back away from a meeting of officers. No disrespect, the club knew of his previous standing with the DMC; he knew what time it was, but protocol is not abandoned just to make a guy feel good about himself. Not in this world.

He determined to allow two hundred dollars to work itself into or out of a larger bankroll, which depended on the temperature of the table and this gambler's discernment. He knew to watch a table to determine if it was cold, warming, or hot. The crowd was the first clue. There were only six people at the table and they were all, judging by the visible chip racks, near death. Nobody there could withstand a couple of bad rolls. Most of them were invested in stupid, high visibility sucker bets. The bigger the area devoted to a certain play, the worse the odds. It was a lure, something to beg the inexperienced players and the drunks who 'feel it' when they toss chips at one-roll bets or promises of big payoffs on single, or low odds numbers.

The dice rule the game, sevens and elevens on the first roll are winners; two, three and twelves spell disaster to the majority of folks who bet with the shooter. The 'Don't' bettors run opposite, but the odds are basically the same. The idea is to establish a point on the first or, 'come out roll' and hit that point, (4,5,6,8,9,10) again before the now dreaded seven rears its ugly head again.

The veteran player will watch a table for a few rolls to determine the climate by the frequency of shooters hitting their intended numbers before the dreaded seven rears its ugly head and wipes out everything. It's glorious!

The preacher stood behind the only guy who appeared to have a clue and watched as three successive points were made. A four, a six, and a nine. The four was the last point made and the trigger for James to toss two crisp one hundred dollar bills at the table boss and request, "change please," which produced a pile of five dollar chips and four twenty-five dollar chips that James quickly pocketed. As the table limit was only five dollars, common for state line tables, James placed two chips on the pass line for the 'come out' roll and handled the remaining chips as he formulated his plan. When the dice came to a quiet standstill in front of

James, he shook his head as he saw a three and a one.

"Four easy, the point is four," the stickman yelled as the shooter continued his hand at the dice. James knew he was up against it as the possibility of another four being made was slim.

As was his custom, he placed bets on the six and the eight, twenty-four dollars each. He backed his pass line bet with the unadvertised double odds bet that mirrored the maximum allowed, his ten dollar pass line bet. The pit boss looked up at him without expression. *These men had no souls*, he thought.

Several harmless numbers — a twelve, a nine, and a five — and the old stirring began. He was not a patient man; he knew also that a seven right now would rip the sixty-eight dollars from his net worth and cause the feeling of worthlessness and failure that all gamblers fight.

The shooter continued throwing numbers and James continued to pile up the winnings. The table had swelled to capacity as thirty minutes of nothing but numbers had positioned the craps table as the focal point of the casino. The players were loud and high-fiving each other with every successful point. It was 'them' against the house and right now the good guys were winning. James was exchanging fives for twenty-fives and twenty-fives for hundreds as his bankroll grew. He knew he was up but had no idea how much. This was fun.

The gaming surface was mayhem. The players were placing every imaginable combination of insane wagers and most of them were paying off. James resisted most of the insanity but pressed his pass line and place bets and also added the four, five, nine, and ten to his placements. This was how to crush the house when the table got hot. It was fast and furious and James wondered how the employees could possibly keep track of all the bets. He was intent and focused on his play and the stick men, even the evil pit bosses held him in respect. This unshaven biker was methodically killing them this morning.

After another point was made, James took a twenty-five dollar chip and placed it next to his 'come out' bet of the same denomination and said, "this is for you, guys," as he looked to the beautiful young blond who had just taken over for the stick man directly across from him. He knew from experience that once the house is on the run like this, the next move is to engage the employees so that they, too, benefit. Now it was everyone against the house and James loved it.

Sure enough, the first roll was a seven and the place went nuts! Everyone was hugging and high-fiving each other; even the pit crew was smiling as the twenty-five became fifty and went into the tip jar. "Thank you, sir," they all said. James pressed his pass line to fifty dollars and did the same for the employees. "Thank you, SIR," they all said in unison.

"It's on now!" James yelled in his first outburst.

"Seven a winner," the stickman yelled again as the dice came to rest showing a five and a two.

"Fifty-two," James yelled as he smacked the big man next to him on the shoulder.

It was then that Kit and Tio showed up.

"You ready to roll out?" Kit asked.

"Are you kidding me?" James asked in disbelief. "Bro, this is the hottest table I've ever seen; I'm thinking about moving here," he yelled.

Tio reached into his buddy's stack of chips and tossed a twenty-five dollar chip and yelled, "Eleven."

James looked at his buddy with wide eyes. "That's a sucker bet, bro. I never bet the eleven."

"It appears that you just did," Kit said laughing.

"There's a reason that bet pays fifteen to one, bro," James lectured.

"Yo, eleven," the stickman yelled.

"Pay up, sucker," Tio demanded. "How much do I get?" he continued.

James looked at Tio, "Dude, that's fifteen to one or ..."

"... three seventy-five Einstein. Give us each a hundred and we'll let you keep playing," Tio laughed.

James handed each of them four twenty-five dollar chips and pocketed the rest. "Better press your eight," Tio said.

"Not yet, bro, I have a system and believe it or not, it's working pretty well right now," he said and turned back to the table.

"Eight the hard way!" exclaimed the blond. James reluctantly turned to acknowledge his friend's second hunch but they were halfway to the cashier already. Preacher laughed out loud; he was thrilled that his friends were cashing in on this roll, too.

Call it another hunch, call it divine intervention, but at that very moment of elation, the preacher felt separated from all that he loved. He recognized, even in the midst of the celebration, that it was fleeting and artificial. The Apostle Paul had written that all things were permissible but not all things were profitable. James knew that there was nothing wrong with a little toss of the dice now and then — nobody's salvation was at issue here — but he could sense the seduction and the lie and he pulled his bets down, assigned his pass line bet to the employees, and walked away from the table. He, James Walters, the suicidal gambler, walked away from a scorching hot table.

As he slowly walked toward the cashier, he heard groans of despair as the table began to claim its victims. Many people pushed everything on the table, blind to the near-empty hourglass, desperate for one more run. Seconds later another loud groan and the death rattle had begun. *As quickly as it comes, it can be taken.* Riches grow wings. The scraggly biker emptied his pockets and claimed his three thousand nine hundred and twenty dollars. Not bad for a two-hundred dollar stake.

CHAPTER TWENTY-THREE

"You guys were just gonna leave me?" James asked as he came up on his brothers at the bikes near the front of the casino. Bike parking had its benefits.

"We told you we were ready; we thought you were gonna move here," Kit laughed.

"And miss the strawberry shake?" James asked. "Not likely, bro. I think I'll even offer to buy today; I did pretty well in there," he added.

"Sinner," Tio said.

"Oh, jeez, here we go," James said. "How did the meeting go with those guys?"

"Waste of time," Kit said. "They've got some stupid ideas; best to leave them where they are."

"Prophets are fine just like we are," Tio added.

The men formed a triangle as James led them in a prayer for safety and ministry; he always asked for ministry opportunities on the road and the Lord never failed to give them some crazy encounters along the way. Diners, tire shops, you name it, these guys have ministered and blessed dozens of motorists and fellow bikers almost everywhere they went. They expected opportunities.

***

The Baker grade on Interstate 15 south was a nasty hill in the desert heat. Thankfully, these guys had ample horsepower to make quick work of this torturous climb. A large twenty-year-old motor home did not enjoy the same trip. James sped up and motioned to his friends that he was pulling over to offer assistance. The three shut down and hit the shoulder quickly, then turned the bikes north and cruised up to the steaming vertical grille of the motor home. The two elderly folks appeared a bit scared of the three mangy-looking bikers walking toward them. The old man emerged from the wheeled fortress first and said, "What's up boys?"

"We just stopped to see if you needed any help," James offered.

"Not unless you guys carry a four hundred dollar radiator and hoses," the man laughed, shaking his head. "Tears into our vacation money a bit, but thankfully there's a mechanic on his way who has just the fix for this old thing," he said.

"Sounds like you're getting the desert house-call rate," Tio said.

"Yeah, but you just gotta be glad there's someone who can get her fixed without towing it a hundred miles for another grand," the man said.

"We don't want no trouble, boys. Really, we're fine; the mechanic should be here any time," the man added nervously.

James reached into his pocket and peeled off five one hundred dollar bills and handed them to the old man. "Take this, should be enough for hoses and some coolant and maybe even a strawberry shake up in Baker," James said, smiling.

The man's wife had gathered enough courage to step down from the old coach and join her husband. "What in heaven's name?" she asked.

"Yes, ma'am, you've got it right. God himself sent us to you today to help you on your way. He just wants you to know that you're always on His mind and that

He loves you and He sent His son to pay a debt that we could not pay and that through faith in Him, you will live forever in heaven with Him; that's the plan." James said.

"Have a nice day," Kit said, as he turned and walked to his bike.

"I don't know what to say; I really can't take your money," the man said.

"We don't even know you," his wife added.

"My name's James, this is Tio, and that was Kit. We're with the Prophets motorcycle club and now you know us and you can very definitely take the money. It was given to us anyway; it's really not ours," he said. "Now enjoy your vacation, enjoy each other, and enjoy what Jesus has done for all of us; trust Him." James walked to his bike.

The three hit the highway and left the dumbfounded senior citizens with a story, not that anyone would ever believe them, but it would be fun to tell it. The bikers smiled big smiles as they looked at each other without a word and continued south in search of the elusive strawberry shake.

***

Six dollars was a ridiculous price for a milkshake, but then again it was ridiculously large. And fresh. And cold. And it was one hundred and seven degrees at one p.m. when the three marauding philanthropists happened upon the very same joint they had stopped at just a few short hours before in search of a breakfast shake. Timing is everything, so they say.

The men found an eight-foot section of shade from a low hanging date palm and huddled together, draining the shakes to their foundations. Hadleys in Cabazon was the only other place where James just had to stop. Oh, and that big fruit stand market place on the 14 just out of Tehachapi, which boasted some amazing lemonade. These stops could keep a man focused on turning some miles just to enjoy some of life's simple pleasures.

Kit and Tio let James pay for the drinks after he convinced them that parting with five hundred an hour earlier was a small percentage of his take from Kate's. They marveled at the speed at which that sum of money was amassed, but James insisted that the dice could reduce a man to wandering through the desert in deep conversation with himself on days that weren't so kind. He just hit a hot table at the right time. It happened sometimes.

It was Kit's turn to spot the blessing. His cup a pointer, he motioned to the young couple hiking up the service drive, both bent and beaten with backpacks. The guy had just handed his walking stick to the lady. It didn't seem to help much. The bikers slowly made their way toward the struggling pair.

"Where you headed?" Kit asked.

"L.A," the young man answered.

"You planning to walk to Los Angeles?" Kit asked.

"We hope not," the girl laughed.

"We've been hitchin' since Salt Lake City. We got a few rides, but we've been walking for a couple of hours this time," he said.

As if by script, the three bikers each produced a one hundred dollar bill, but Kit said, "Oh no, this one is mine; put those away."

"Let me do half at least," Tio argued.

"Find your own; these two are mine," Kit barked.

James quietly returned his money to his pocket.

"And you," Kit said, nodding to the preacher. "You can't pay for anything else today after that last stunt," Kit demanded.

The two hikers were quietly but nervously looking at one another.

"There's a bus station next to that milkshake place."

"Which we highly recommend by the way," Tio interrupted.

"The milkshake, not the bus; we don't know about the busses," James said.

"Just take the money and get a bus ticket to Los Angeles. It's air-conditioned and you can rest up," Kit finished.

"Please take the money. He'll get all mad and take it out on us if you don't," James said.

The guy tentatively reached toward Kit's heavily tattooed arm and gently took the bill. "We appreciate it very much. I really don't know what to say."

"Do you guys know that Jesus is alive and well and that He loves you?" James asked.

"We do now," the young lady laughed.

"Yeah, well, He is and He does," he finished and handed her his card. "If you're ever around Berdoo on Saturday nights, we have a little church over that way and we'd love to have you visit."

"Okay, thanks; really, thanks very much. You're like big hairy angels or something," she laughed again.

"God bless you guys," Kit said.

The two moved considerably quicker as they left the three crazy guys and headed to the bus station.

CHAPTER TWENTY-FOUR

There's no better feeling than a nice long shower after a ride like that. Freaking hot out there and the highway just pounds you into submission on a long trip. The hot water served to loosen every stiff joint in his fifty-one year old frame. He felt amazingly good and the prospect of dinner with his beautiful fiancée buoyed his mood further. His only trepidation came in the form of the realization that he needed to level with Linda regarding his accident and the potential danger of hanging around him. He knew he had waited too long to tell her, which was also a problem. Oh well, he had to deal with it and let the chips fall where they may. Still, he'd rather be center-punched than sit across from a scorned female. As a couple, they'd miraculously survived several months without a major fight and he had fantasized about a conflict-free marriage. *As long as she did what he said, things would be fine,* he kidded to himself.

After drying off and sliding into a clean pair of jeans, he checked his phone. He'd missed a call during his mental sojourn to marital lala land. Gordon had called so the preacher hit the number and while it rang, hoped that Gordo had some interesting news.

"James, hey, I just finished up everything and you were right, the substance on the tire came from that exact oiler, or at least from a similar truck with the same brand of oil," he said.

"Wow, well I guess that's at least grounds to pursue the theory further," James mused.

"So how do you want me to handle this; just call the cop who gave you his card?" Gordon asked.

"I don't know; let me think on this for a couple of hours. I have to seek counsel on this one, Gordo. I appreciate your help and yes, I'll call you as soon as I decide how to handle this. We're pretty good little amateur detectives there, brotha," James said.

"Amateur? I beg to differ," he laughed.

"Thanks again; I'll call you in a bit," James said.

"Happy to help," Gordon said.

***

James hated drama, but he found himself smack in the middle of a crime story and the pending scolding from his bride-to-be. Not a good situation. He couldn't tell Snake yet. That would cause a war inside the DMC — not that it wouldn't be fun to watch from afar — but it would have to wait. What was Cedar's angle? What was the motivation? How would he gain if Snake was six feet under? And who nominated this preacher to figure it all out?

He should call Kit, but as with Linda, he feared reprisal. Kit would rightfully ask him just what the heck he was doing; this was DMC business and playing politics in the biker world was a great way to get his head kicked in — from his own brothers! No telling what the DMC would do to him if they knew what he was up to. *Got to get a handle on this*, he thought. He dialed Kit's number. To his surprise, Kit listened intently with only a couple of one-word interruptions to voice his disbelief on a couple of points. When he finished his summary, he paused and asked his 'P' what he would do if he were in the same spot.

Kit said, "I wouldn't be in the same spot," and laughed.

James was relieved to hear his friend and president laugh. They decided that James needed to hand it all off to Gordon and let him contact the police. There was no way, no freaking way that a Prophet was going to call in the cops, no matter what. "We take care of our own business, bro; this ain't our business," Kit said. James agreed but pushed the envelope a bit with the question of who should tell Snake.

Kit didn't hesitate. "You need to tell him everything you know and suspect and why and then walk away. Do not get involved any further if you want to keep those colors on your back; you understand me? I get it that Snake is a brother and you need to protect him by telling him what you know and think, but that's it, bro; this is DMC business. Tell me you understand this."

"I'm pickin' up what you're throwin' down, bro; you have my word," answered James.

"I don't need to say this, but I'm gonna," Kit continued. "Not a word to anyone in our club, bro; not a word from you — you copy?"

"Not a word," James agreed.

"This is gonna get crazy, bro," Kit said. "This jerk Cedar has something going on. It smells like a takeover, but from what you tell me, this guy doesn't have the juice to pull it off himself so either some other DMC are involved or he's a plant and he's working with another club. This ain't the Feds; they can't 'off' dudes, at least not now. That could change, of course; they make the rules.

"Dang, bro," he said, "The more I think about this, this could get nuts," Kit laughed.

"Guess we just sit back and make some popcorn," James said.

"No doubt," Kit said. "Okay, bro, keep me posted, but get this over as soon as you can. We need to move away from this before the you-know-what hits the fan."

"Amen, bro; I need to get out of the CSI business and back to bikin' and preachin'," said James. "It was fun, though, except for the doberman." They both laughed.

CHAPTER TWENTY-FIVE

Linda answered the door with a smile that got bigger when she saw the flowers.

"Oh wow, those are beautiful! What's the occasion ... what did you do?" she said with that little squint, rendering him helpless. She was beautiful in a thousand ways.

"What did I do? I just wanted to surprise you with flowers," James said as innocently as possible.

"Uh huh. Okay, come on in," she said as she kissed him.

"You smell incredible," he said.

"I know," she teased.

They settled onto the overstuffed sofa next to the sliding screen door that led to a patio straight out of *Coastal Living*. At this time of day the gentle breeze distributes the jasmine throughout the room and makes for a delicious place to hang out and talk. Linda had spent every day of the six years since buying the place in that patio garden laying pavers, building trellises, planting dwarf citrus trees, and adding the most beautiful and aromatic flowers and bushes available. It was a paradise minutes from civilization. James loved it there; it was the only place he could truly relax and become remotely vulnerable. That was about to end.

Linda's perfect green eyes narrowed as he told her the story of the Saturday morning shotgun blast.

"I should have told you when it happened, but I didn't want you to worry," he said.

"You didn't tell me because it was inconvenient for you to tell me. You knew I would tell you how insane this all is and you didn't want to hear that."

"I don't blame …"

"Don't patronize me, James. You think this is funny and if you just bring me flowers and feed me your story I'll say okay, honey, no problem, I'm here for you no matter what. But I'm not going there, James; it's not okay. You want to risk your life being big bad biker, go ahead, but count me out! How dare you not tell me this! How dare you put me in harm's way by letting me go through the past week with calliopes playing in my head thinking that everything's wonderful, my fiancée loves me and puts my safety above everything else," she said as her voice broke. Tears filled her eyes and she turned away.

"You knew who I was when you went out with me; you know this life brings some weird stuff. I'm out of the outlaw world, I'm serving the Lord, I'm try …"

"Spare me the 'I'm trying' speech, James; it's not about you. I know that's hard for you to hear, but you're not the lone wolf tough guy anymore; you've got me and you're still running around like an outlaw! I'm not going to live like this," she whispered.

"I'm sorry I didn't tell you, but I didn't shoot myself off the, bike, Linda. I was riding up to Big Bear to write a sermon. I screwed up not telling you but …"

"But? I tell you if I miss a left turn on the way to work, I tell you what I'm buying at the store, there's nothing I don't tell you. I can't believe how selfish you are sometimes. I feel like a complete fool. Everything is transparent with me. What *else* aren't you telling me?"

"Aww, Linda, don't go there. Jeez, look at me; I walked away from the DMC, I joined a freaking Christian club, I'm trying to serve God …"

"I know all that, James; you've made your 'poor me, I quit the DMC, now I'm just a humble preacher' point several times. I get it. It's a good thing, but this is not some door prize. God got you out of that madness! Why you can't just receive that for the blessing it is and quit with the 'I gave so much up to serve the Lord' routine?"

He saw the futility of his argument. "You're right. You usually are, and I love that about you. I knew you'd be upset and I am selfish and I didn't tell you because I didn't want to hear this, even though you're right. It was wrong to endanger you by keeping you in the dark. I don't want to lose you. I guess that's the bottom line. I'm sorry," he said.

"You got a minute? I've got some more to tell you," he said sheepishly.

"Oh my gosh, James, what else? Get it all out; tell me whatever you have to tell me and then leave, please. I can't live like this; I'm serious," she surrendered.

"I already told you I didn't believe Snake's crash was an accident. I have a theory that it's connected to the same guy who had me shot. When I went to the hospital to see Snake, this guy and Bones came at me and I kinda took both of them out. Magic was there, and nothing else happened, but this one guy, Cedar, didn't just shake hands and let it go. I think he set me up on the run up the hill."

Linda was slowly shaking her head.

"I'm not done. The oil on the road where Snake when down was put there by an oiler truck from the paving company that Cedar works for. I think he's behind the Snake crash; I think he's a plant from another club trying to get rid of Snake and take over the DMC. You know Gordon from church?"

Linda nodded. "What does he have to do with all of this craziness?"

"Well, he's a chemist. He teaches at UCR and he did an analysis of the oil from Snake's front tire and from the oiler truck and they are one-and-the-same. A perfect match."

"How did Gordon get oil from some truck?" she asked.

"I hopped the fence last night and grabbed a sample for him to test. He did the tests while I ran up to Stateline with Kit and Tio. Gordon called me a little while ago and confirmed that it's the same stuff. Now he's going to the cops with the whole thing gift-wrapped for those idiots. All I need to do now is tell Snake the whole story and I'm done. I promised Kit and I'm promising you. I'm done."

"So am I, James. All that you've told me is foreign crazy talk to me. I know it's your world, but it's not mine and it will never be mine. I'm sorry. I *do* love you, but I can't live in constant worry and fear," she sobbed, now well past keeping her cool. "My God, James, all that you've done here has outlaw written all over it. You got into a fight at the hospital and you broke into a business to steal a sample of oil to prove an attempted murder. HELLO! Am I the only one who thinks this is a bit *out there*?"

"It wasn't much of a fight," he said with a smile, employing his patented charm, "and I didn't break into anything. I jumped over the fence and swabbed the spray nozzle of a truck."

She just stared at him.

James continued. "Somebody tried to kill my friend, baby girl, and if I can do something about it, I will," he barked.

"That's something for the police, James; that's how civilized people deal with crime!" she yelled.

"Excuse me ... the police? Are you serious? They're not the least bit concerned with Snake, or me, or anything to do with us; they hope we kill each other off. They don't believe the church is a church, they watch me like a felon; we don't call the cops!"

"They watch you like a felon? Maybe that's because you *are* a felon!" she screamed.

"You don't know anything about that, you hear me? Nothing! And you sure don't know me," he yelled as he side-armed the flowers across the coffee table. "I've had enough judgment from you, Miss Perfect. Go find some phony cheap suit banker; they're all so proper and honest!"

CHAPTER TWENTY-SIX

His righteous anger lasted a whole two blocks before the self-loathing kicked in. This was all spiritual warfare, but neither recognized it as the conversation morphed into argument, then all-out fight, complete with misplaced anger and fear and insecurities. Isn't that the way it goes? We only hurt the ones we love?

Linda wasn't doing much better as she picked up the flowers that hadn't hit the waste basket and held them to her chest as she leaned, exhausted, against the kitchen counter. She knew by the sound of that motorcycle that he was beyond mad; he was hurt. She hurt him with her words when all of her reasoning skills were bankrupted against his thick skull. She resorted to cutting remarks designed not to score debate points like she masterfully did in college, but to lash out and hurt him. She was right, of course; her pride certainly told her that. He had no right to put her in danger by not telling her; at least she would have been able to make decisions armed with that knowledge.

***

The cigar lounge at the ritzy River shopping plaza in Palm Desert was empty, save a well-dressed octogenarian sitting on a stool carefully lighting what appeared to be a maduro-wrapped Toro size cigar.

James nodded to the older gentleman. "What kind of cigar is that? It looks perfect to me right about now."

"CAO Brazilia, young man, and I would have to agree with you; it's about to be perfect," he laughed.

"Mind if I join you?" James asked.

"Not at all son; go get your cigar. I'll be here enjoying this one."

Before prison, the preacher smoked six hundred dollars worth of fine cigars every month. He and Snake enjoyed a smoke almost nightly at the DMC clubhouse while pounding beers or sipping whiskey with any number of Doomsayers. If it sounds decadent, it's only because it was. Prison allowed for none of these fleshly pleasures and after his release, the urge to smoke was gone, along with the one for drink. Since then he'd only had a handful of cigars and no drink, thank God. That would ruin everything and he knew it.

There were times that the thought of riding away for a few days and going totally off the reservation had appealed to him, but reason and the Holy Spirit kept him sane. James knew the devil was a worthy adversary. He kept in mind never to get too hungry, angry, lonely, or tired. *Well*, he thought, as he ceremoniously lit the cigar, *at least I'm not tired.*

"James," he said, and stuck out his hand.

"Irving, Irving Rosenthal," the man said and shook it.

"Well, Irving, I compliment you on your choice of stick. I love maduros and this one is amazingly smooth for the price. I've had pricier smokes that were not nearly as good. This tastes like a chocolate bar," James laughed.

"Ah, simple pleasures, James; don't give them all up," he said.

"You're looking quite dapper there, Irving, if you don't mind me saying so."

"Thank you," he said as he respectfully bowed his head. "It's my Friday night ritual since my wife died," he added.

"I'm sorry for your loss; how long has it been?"

"Seven years now; seems like yesterday," his voice faded.

"We never forget; the pain never goes away," James said as Irving looked quizzically at his new friend. "Michelle died … years ago now and not only do I not go a day without feeling the loss, I compare every other woman I meet to her."

Irving nodded and smiled knowingly. "I know the feeling," he said.

James smiled and then laughed out loud and said, "She pissed me off more than any other human being I've ever known and now I only remember her as a saint," to which both men laughed until they coughed. "She was perfect, Irv!"

"My wife could piss off Mother Theresa," Irving laughed. "She drove me nuts, especially about these," he said as he waved the cigar around. "I love you,

Cynthia, but I'm smokin' my butt off down here," Irving continued. "She's up there right now telling God, 'Are you just gonna let him get away with this? He's mocking me, you know; what are you going to do with him?' I can just hear God saying 'Oy Vay, enough of you already.'"

The two laughed and shared small talk for a few minutes when Irving asked, "So what brings you to Palm Desert on a Friday night? Where's your date? It's date night, you know."

"I had a date; in fact, I had a fiancée up until a couple hours ago. We had a big fight and here I am," James answered.

"Ah, the carelessness of youth," Irving said.

"I like hanging with you, Irving; you think I'm young," James laughed.

"You are young. How old are you?"

"Fifty-one," James said.

Irving chuckled. "I had already finished a military career when you were in fifth grade, my friend; you are indeed young. Call her and tell her you're sorry," the old man suggested.

"Why am I sorry? She said some pretty hurtful things. I'm not so sure about the whole thing at this point," James said defensively.

"Tell me," Irving changed the subject. "What does this jacket mean; you're a biker, yes?"

"Yes sir, the jacket, the vest, what we call a "cut"; these are our colors, the Prophets motorcycle club. We're Christians; this is our ministry," James said.

"I see," the old man answered as he turned his cigar and savored with his eyes closed. "So you believe that Jesus is the Messiah?"

"Yes sir, I do," James said.

"I do as well, although it wasn't always that way," Irving said.

"You're Jewish, aren't you?" James asked.

"Yes, from a proud lineage," Irving laughed. "It was my wife who showed me the ancient scriptures in a new light. I saw clearly how the prophecies pointed to

Jesus as the Christ, but you must understand that for a Jew to convert, it means losing family and friends, much more I dare say than when the Gentiles repent from their unbelief, although I know you face ridicule as well," he said.

"Sure we do, but who cares? I mean really, Irv, in the grand scheme of things, who really cares what a bunch of people think when it comes to salvation of one's soul?"

"Indeed. The bottom line, as you would say," Irving said.

"The bottom line is, what does God say about it?" James added.

"Good point, my young friend; God's word is the final arbiter in all matters," the old man said.

"Cheers," James said and tilted his cigar toward his new friend.

The elder looked at his new friend for a minute and then smiled. James smiled and closed his eyes, enjoying his smoke.

Irving broke the silence.

"You said fiancée; that is serious business, young man. Surely you don't base the prospects of your future together on one disagreement?"

"You wouldn't think so," James said.

"You two will work things out," the old man said.

"Hard to say right now, Irv; she was pretty tired of my routine an hour ago." James smiled.

"You should call her and tell her you love her and that you're sorry for your part in all of this," Irving said.

"What? Not so fast, Irv; she needs some time to feel some of this, too," James said defensively.

"Ah, I see; you need to make your point," he said.

"I'm just saying it's not all me."

"It never is, but who really cares who pushes the first domino if the end result is reconciliation and restoration?" Irving said. "What does our Lord say about 'self,' James?" Irving continued before James

224

could answer; "He says we are to die to our self, die to our flesh. Do you agree?"

James looked at the old guy with the look of a chess player who had been backed into inevitable checkmate. "Yes, it says that," James admitted.

"Then how can a dead man have hurt feelings?"

The two men sat in silence as plumes of aromatic smoke drifted overhead. "You will be a good husband once again, James; you are just struggling with the old self and the spiritual new creation. Remember that the word of God says that a husband must love his wife as Christ loved the church," he continued. James slowly turned to Irving when the old man finished with, "and the last time I checked, that cost Him dearly."

"I appreciate your counsel, Irving; you're a good man, a wise man. I'm honored to make your acquaintance. I will strongly consider your words," James said. "A dapper guy like yourself must have many ladies chasing you around," he kidded his new friend.

"You're too kind. There have been a couple of wonderful ladies who have expressed interest in my company but I, unlike you, don't feel anything near the love which is required for a proper attempt at any relationship beyond my Cynthia," Irving said quietly.

"My wife used to say there's a lid for every pot, Irving; I think someone might be out there for you," he encouraged.

"I've heard that said, but consider this, my friend; maybe some pots are constructed as to be so custom that only one lid will match it," the old man said, "and when that lid is broken or lost, that's it for the pot."

"Maybe it's not custom from the factory but the dents and dings of life have so shaped us that nothing fits anymore," James suggested. They both laughed.

As enjoyable as Irving and the cigar were, the road was calling again. One thing hadn't changed, James' inability to just relax for more than an hour, anywhere. He thought he was getting better at it but he was just an active thinker and that led to new ideas and off he went. Simple really. He bid farewell to his new friend and mentioned that if this was a regular stop for Irving, maybe they'd meet up again soon. They shook hands and thanked each other for the conversation and the fellowship. James mentioned the church and handed Irving a card as an invitation in the event the old man was ever sixty miles west on a Saturday night.

Once seated on the bike, James pulled his phone from his pocket and checked the screen in hopes that Linda had called. She hadn't. Irving's voice was still echoing in his head when he texted, "I love you. Sorry for my part in this, the biggest part" and tucked the phone back in his cut. It was dark now, time for the clear glasses and the anticipation of a great ride back to the shop. Church the next night; gotta get somewhat ready.

CHAPTER TWENTY-SEVEN

Traffic was light, most of it going the other way on a Friday night. As he rode, James thought about Irving and how it might not be so great being alone at eighty-something but that the Lord had been gentle with the old man. Then out of left field came the scripture from Hebrews about watching for opportunities to serve, as you never know when you're entertaining angels. *Ya think?* James thought. *Nah, couldn't be,* he decided and then laughed out loud. *Do angels smoke cigars?*

The bike was incredible. If it weren't for the effortless run past Highway 62 and the long pulling grade to Banning, James would have been considerably more depressed as his mind replayed the fight with Linda. He found it staggering that two people who were in love could go that bad that fast. It had to be spiritual warfare and the two of them walked right into it. Let that be a lesson, he thought: *right when you think you've got it figured out, right when you feel you're bulletproof, you're toast.*

With the engine officially broken in, James was pushing it pretty hard through Banning and Beaumont, laughing to himself about his late wife's hatred of 'B' towns, as they always reminded her of heat and wind. She hated the wind. Barstow, Banning, Beaumont, Baker, Bakersfield, to name a few. He always countered with, "What about Beverly Hills and Bel Air?" and they would laugh. He was running between a hundred and a hundred five through Cherry Valley, past the familiar Live Oak exit where he found his friend 'Tucson' after a horrific wreck the night of Nine Ball's welcome home party, almost a year ago. He smiled as he thought of leading his dying buddy to the Lord on that cold, dark street, the flashing red and blue lights searing the scene into his consciousness.

Chet's shop lights were visible from the freeway so James shut 'er down and took the off ramp. Chet was always good for a cold Coke in a bottle. The guy was so old school; he had a vintage Coca Cola machine with the vertical side door that showed the tops of the bottles through the glass. It was much like Chet — old but quite functional. It wouldn't be cool just passing by without saying 'Hi,' James thought.

The front door was shut, but he could see most of the lights were still on inside so he rolled around back to the shop entrance. Chet had the big doors open, inviting the cooling evening air to ruffle shop manuals and toss the occasional receipt in any direction. Chet was oblivious to the papers as he cussed out an old four-speed transmission he had successfully pulled from a late seventies shovelhead that was waist high on the lift.

"Late night surgery, Chet?" James asked.

"Hey Nine; what's up, brother?" Chet gave his old friend a good strong hug.

"Not much, bro, just finishing the break in on this engine and saw your lights on," he said.

"Glad you stopped, bro; wanna coke?"

"Oh yeah, I was thinkin' of how the cold bottle would feel from a half a mile out," he laughed.

"Get me one while you're in there," Chet said.

James popped both tops with a practiced pull on the side-mounted bottle opener. "I love these, bro; there just ain't nothin' like a cold coke from a bottle."

"You ain't lyin," Chet agreed. They touched the bottles together.

"Cheers," James said. They both took a long pull and simultaneously let out an *ahhhhh* as the refreshment poured.

"Nothing like that battery acid tang," Chet laughed.

"I'm with ya," James said, admiring the bottle. "Old school," he added.

"Speaking of old school, I'm glad you stopped by, bro. I've been thinking of something for a few days that just ain't sittin' right in my old brain," Chet said.

"Talk to me," James answered.

"Well, you remember that tire of Snake's I give ya the other day?"

"No, what tire?" James said with a smile.

"Screw you, Nine, I ain't that old. That DMC punk what dropped it off … whazzis name?"

"Cedar," James answered.

"Yeah, Cedar, he's a punk; more like a branch," Chet laughed. "Guy like him never wears a patch in my day, you know what I'm sayin'?" he said.

"I'm with ya; go on," James said.

"Well, he's walkin' around actin all bad, talking on his little phone, tellin' me what's up in my shop and I'm just lookin' at him thinkin' I'd like to take a bat to his …"

"Is this a long story?" James asked, smiling again.

"You shut the heck up and listen. You came here remember? I didn't freaking invite you here; drink my coke and give me crap?" Chet complained.

James laughed and said, "Go on, I won't interrupt again."

"Anyhow, he was wanderin' in and out and talkin' and I can hear him talkin' about MF'ers this and MF'ers that and I'm thinking it didn't sound right what he was saying. It was like … "when the MFers this and that," not like he was calling anyone an MFer; you follow me?"

James nodded.

"Now ain't the MF'ers a club from the Northwest?" he asked.

"Yeah, they're the Merchants of Fear. They're pretty big up that way and over toward Chicago, but you know they ain't goin' quite to Chi town, not with them other guys up that way," James said.

"Yeah," Chet said. "They ain't that big and bad, huh?"

"Very few are," James said.

Chet went on for a few more minutes, mostly berating Cedar but James was already well past this conversation, pulling the icing recipe out and spreading it on the conspiracy cake.

"You listenin'," Chet asked,

"Yeah; you said Cedar was frontin' you off about listenin' to his phone call," James recovered.

"Yeah, but you know me, I can't hear nothing so I tells him that, and I think he forgot about it, but you know he's got a big mouth and he's stupid ..."

"And ugly," James laughed.

Chet ignored him and said, "So I know better than to be sayin' anything, but then I say to myself, *I ain't getting any younger and I like Snake and you, you guys are old school, and I just thought I should say somethin'.* I just don't feel like this idiot is up to any good, you know?" Chet finished. "And you ain't DMC anymore, so this is like I'm just at the confession booth, you know, preacher? It's like that attorney-client privilege thing — priest/sinner — same thing," said Chet.

"I'm a preacher, not a priest; you ain't gotta tell me nothin'. Jesus paid for your sins at the cross, bro; you just gotta put some faith in that and let him in," James said, never one to miss a shot at bringing a heathen into the fold.

"So you keep tellin' me," Chet said.

"It's never too late, Chet; don't make much sense not taking advantage of the greatest gift in the history of mankind. But you take your time, old man; you'll live forever one way or another. I'd just like to see you with the good guys, that's all," James said. "Come to church, Chet, just one time; honor me, humor me," he laughed.

"You never know," Chet said.

The two men sat in silence for a few minutes. It wasn't uncomfortable, just two guys enjoying a coke. What needed to be said was said and neither of these guys wasted too many words.

"I gotta get back, got a sermon to write; thanks for the beverage, it hit the spot. I'll tell Snake to keep his eyes open. He's getting better; he's made a miraculous comeback so far," James said.

"I heard that yesterday; pretty amazing," said Chet.

"It's that God thing I've been telling you about," James patted his friend on the shoulder.

"Take care, Nine."

"See you 'round, Chet."

CHAPTER TWENTY-EIGHT

"Yeah," the weak voice answered.

"Snake, it's Nine ... I mean Preacher. How you doin'; did I wake you?"

"Of course you woke me, you idiot. I'm in bed all day and night, all I do is sleep. I gotta get outta here, bro. Bust me out; nobody else has the stones. I swear this club is going soft," he laughed.

"You feeling okay? What are the doctors saying?" James asked.

"Best I can figure is I'm out on Monday. See I got great insurance through work and these parasites are billin' up a storm in here," Snake laughed.

"Make sure you order up some quality room service before you roll out," James said.

"Oh, I've tried, but they shot down all my requests for scotch, cigars, dancers ... it's hell in here, bro."

"Savages," James said. "Tell them you are seeking better accommodations first of the week."

"Good advice. So what's up? To what do I owe this phone call? Surely you have better things to do on a Friday night ... where's Linda? It is Friday, right?" Snake asked.

"All night long," James said. "And no, I have nothing better to do, and who are you, Dr. Phil?" he finished.

"You're boring, she should dump you," Snake replied.

"I am what I am, and I think she did earlier this evening," Preacher said.

"Oh, my bad, bro; sorry about that."

"Yeah, me, too. I had it coming, but they do tend to get overly dramatic over little stuff," James said, buffering his own culpability.

"Word. Well, I'm sure you can charm her back to the dark side," Snake joked.

"We shall see."

Preacher spilled everything to Snake, took him through the home-grown crime scene investigation, being careful to leave Gordon's name out of it, alluding to his accomplice only by credentials. Snake loved the part about the doberman and thanked Preacher for all the work.

Things got a little heated when he told him about Cedar and his allegations surrounding the Merchants of Fear. James feared he might be giving his friend a little too much information, considering his fragile condition, but Snake had to know, and he definitely had to know before he left the safety of a guarded hospital room.

Snake mulled the MF'ers situation over and allowed that it was at least possible. One thing, Snake was proud and any insinuation that he had lost control of his club would be met with violent denial. James was very careful to dance around that scenario by allowing Snake to deduce much of the potential for himself. Snake might be proud, but he wasn't stupid and he wasn't blind. The preacher feared that this would pull Snake far into the vengeance and violence that permeates the outlaw culture and if that happened, there was no telling when or if he could pull himself out.

Next came the hard part. James had been instructed in no uncertain terms to walk away from the situation as soon as he had imparted everything he knew to Snake. Kit was not one to mess with either and the preacher did not want to end up a man without a country. He was torn. He had sworn an oath of allegiance to the Doomsayers many years ago. He had upheld every bit of it, including serving three years in prison to protect the club. The older brothers knew what time it was with Nine Ball. It was the young guns who had no respect for him now that he was out. The preacher's pride was in check most of the time, but lately he'd been feeling a bit disrespected and a big part of him wanted to do some damage out there for no other reason than to upgrade his legacy. He knew this was his flesh, he knew it was spiritual warfare, and he was treading too close to the edge on this one.

The fight with Linda, the pending DMC war, at least internally, and quite possibly with the MF'ers acted as a carrot in front of this dumb donkey. He was entertaining some insanely rough and highly unsanctioned thoughts. It was as if, and this might sound weird, but it was like he was meeting with the devil behind God's back. Only problem with that thinking is that God is Omniscient, Omnipresent, and Omnipotent and neither the Preacher nor the devil possessed any of these attributes. Dumb creatures, these humans.

James knew he was on thin ice, but there seemed to be some genetic predisposition toward bad judgment. Like he ate a big bowl of 'Stupid Flakes' for breakfast. Like, why do people always head up the stairs when being chased? Don't they know that at some point they will reach the roof and have to jump somewhere? James hated those movies.

"What do you need me to do?" James asked.

"Nothing, bro; you've done enough and I appreciate everything. Believe me, nobody I have moves or thinks like you do, bro. You are sorely missed but, and dig this, this ain't no dis, but you ain't DMC anymore, bro; we will handle this," Snake said.

"You know I'm right, too, so don't start with the lawyer routine. You're a down brother, you've always been there for me, but I am not allowing you anywhere near this. I don't need God pissed at me. You've got your path, now walk it; show the rest of us the way. I'll catch up later."

"Fine by me, bro, I don't need the drama. I'm just not too good at walking away from stuff like this ..."

"Oh, I know that!" Snake laughed. "You've got plenty of priors for gettin' busy."

"Get yourself a copy of the security tapes at Four Seasons Paving for the night you crashed; see if that truck went out after hours. My guess is that it did and if so ..."

"Okay, Sherlock, I got it; we'll take it from here, bro," Snake said.

The preacher knew his friend was right; he knew his own judgment was currently existing in a compromised state. He was also coming to realize that he didn't trust or believe that he was worthy of living above the fray, that maybe he sabotaged every good thing that God tossed his way, that there was some weird pathology at work here. Fear of success? This foray into psychoanalysis would have to wait; the only couch he'd be employing would be in his own office tonight after an exhaustive marathon of A.W. Tozer lectures.

He agreed, at least for the night, to abide with the wishes of his current and former presidents. This wasn't over by a long shot and his unwillingness to bow out gracefully should have been cause for concern, but as usual, James thought he knew best. Even in the face of this, the scripture was playing in his head, "Lean not on your own understanding." You'd think he'd listen. Like an athlete who's been forced out of the game, he missed the lights and the rush of competition. Sometimes we're the last to realize that the game, or the career, or the relationship, has passed us by. Here's where trust comes in; we need to trust God, not just believe in God. Belief won't get us saved. The devil believes all day long but he's not put any trust in God; it's all about him, always has been. He spends his day trying to get us to fall for the same line. Remember in Genesis, 'you can be like God,' he said. Liar.

The preacher was fascinated by what Snake said regarding walking his path and he'd catch up later.

Seems God will use whatever He needs to use to get us to hear His voice. The calling was loud and clear; he was pulled out of that lifestyle to lead others to Christ. Like the adage, James found himself 'lonely at the top.' He was a leader, he'd been chosen to blaze the trail, and the minutes after the phone call were filled with reassurances from scripture and from the spirit of God. 'To whom much is given, much will be required,' 'Whom shall I send?' James bowed his head before his Lord and whispered, "Here am I."

His sanity was returning, and with it his joy. Knowing that he was smack dab in the middle of God's will is an electrifying place to be. James felt blessed and loved and home, that peace he'd felt on occasion, the one the Bible calls the 'peace which passes all understanding,' was upon him once again. God was faithful. He prayed for Linda. He prayed that if they were supposed to be together God would make a way. God's will, that was the extent of this preacher's prayer life anymore. Oh sure, there was a laundry list of stuff he asked God, but now everything was prefaced by,

"Your will, Lord," because at the end of the day, that's what he wanted. "Not my will, but yours be done."

The Bible says we've already been given all we need for life and godliness so what the heck are we doing rubbing the God lamp and asking for a bunch of weird stuff like a little kid before Christmas. 'Delight yourself in the Lord and He will give you the desires of your heart.' Do we trust Him or not? If we trust God, then we should be quite content to let Him be the provider, let Him choose; we don't know better! We may think we know, but as they say in A.A., our best thinking got us here!

James laughed to himself as he rested in the Lord's grace and mercy. He was thankful to be alive and healthy and as his buddy once said, if we all gathered at a big round table and tossed our problems out and could switch with anyone else we'd all end up taking back our own problems and just dealing with life. At least we're familiar with our own issues.

CHAPTER TWENTY-NINE

His landlord's VW bug was parked at the side of the building, which meant old Bud was roaming around somewhere. Maybe he was finally getting to the warehouse outside lights that had only worked intermittently since James took the building at Christmas last year. Had it only been six months?

Recliner or couch? Tough decision. He opted for the comfort of the chair, thinking it would be more suitable for finishing a great book by A.W. Tozer that he'd started reading about a week ago and could base some of Saturday's sermon on several of the great thoughts contained within. His father used to have a favorite recliner and as a child there was always a peace in the house when dad was in his chair. All was right with the world. With that sweet memory came the devil right behind with, 'too bad you never had kids; you'll die alone and nobody will care.'

Man, this guy is relentless; I'll give him that. James shook that thought from his head. He and Michelle had discussed kids and were about ready when the cancer came. "Dang it," James said out loud, slamming his book down. With one motion, he rocked the chair upright and headed to the refrigerator for an iced tea. *Maybe I do need the shrink's couch tonight after all,* he thought as he reached for his favorite glass.

Once again he settled into the chair and once again his study was interrupted by his out-of-control brain. 'God has not given us the spirit of fear,' and something about 'a sound mind,' but James was questioning Him about that one right now. All he could think about was Linda and what she was doing and why wasn't she as miserable as he was. He replayed the fight, felt bad about leaving the way he did and losing his temper, but really, it wasn't that bad of a fight. He rationalized for a few minutes before admitting to God and himself that it wasn't the fight that distanced her, it was his seeming disregard for her safety. He'd kept arguing that he'd protect and defend her to his death and she kept saying if he wouldn't place her in these situations or positions, he wouldn't have to. They'd gone back and forth. He just didn't listen. He heard her now. He missed her and dang it, he needed her. Boy, did he hate that realization.

Balance. Always seek balance. God had taught him years ago, even before he had acknowledged God, that placing another human being in front of Him was always a bad move. We need to seek God first and He will add everything else. We always try it the other way around. Seek things, then after we have all we want, go looking for God to rubber stamp our stupid lives. That's the enemy's plan, not God's. When we have a personal relationship with the living God through His son Jesus Christ, we are never alone and we never 'need' anything or anyone else. God is always there. He won't die from cancer and he won't run off with a younger model. He's been telling us all along that we need to put Him first and once that's handled, He will meet all of our needs.

James knew this and lived this pretty well after his release from prison left him alone for a year or so. God became his source, things were ordered; then along came Linda and it seemed that she was part of the plan. James certainly hoped that he was part of the plan for her life, too. They had sought God in prayer together, and individually, they honored God by planning a marriage, not just shacking up. Maybe they just needed a couple of days to sort this out and be sure they both had God in the number one spot.

Reading Tozer only served to remind James that he wasn't all that smart. This guy was a genius and his writing, though detailed and deep, was palatable. James was eating this stuff up. Sipping on an iced tea and reading theology in his comfortable chair brought a smile to his face as he contrasted his earlier desire to engage in some outlaw biker war with his current position. Talk about extremes. He extended the recliner to its full degree of comfort. He could sleep right there until morning. *Who needed a bed when he had this thing?*

James gently laid the book down on his chest, turned his head, and sniffed the air; he thought he detected a decidedly electric taste in the air. *Must be Bud*, he thought and he continued reading. Ten minutes passed and the smell persisted, even stronger. He thought to get up but decided to call Bud's cell phone instead. As he reached for his phone the fire alarm jarred him from his peace. He had only heard that sound once before when the fire department was granting his occupancy. It seemed twice as loud now as it pierced the quiet evening.

His call to Bud went unanswered. After the voicemail did its thing, James yelled into the phone, "Bud, what the hell is going on? Call me, the fire alarm is going off." By the time he got up and reached the office door, the smell was acrid and upon opening, overwhelming. The hallway lights were on but he couldn't see the stairs, which were only fifteen feet away, so he ducked back into his office for some air. If he was going to make a run for it, he would have to do it from memory. He stood there for a minute, thought of Linda, and made his decision. He asked the Lord for guidance and wisdom, took a deep breath, and opened the door.

He was met by a blast of heat that knocked him against the wall. It was intense and with tightly closed eyes, he ran toward the stairway, his hand against the wall to feel the edge that would guide him down the flight of stairs to the lobby. From his many trips up and down those steps, he knew there were eighteen of them and his mind's eye provided a perfect picture from which to work.

The fire was loud. He could hear walls and beams crashing down and a weird rushing sound, like a fountain filling the air. He yelled Bud's name, but heard only the cacophony of destruction. Should he have stayed in his office longer? Should he have called the fire department first? All this ran through his mind as he reached out for the first step. "God please save me," he screamed in his mind as he realized there was no guarantee that the first floor was a safe destination. He was going for the front door; he had made his decision and he was too far now. He counted seven steps and then a sickening feeling of falling helplessly, arms and legs now flailing, as he braced himself for the impact which should be ... *where was the floor?*

His mind was paralyzed with fear as he kept falling; it had to have been ten seconds now, still falling, darker and hotter. "God, I can't breathe, the heat is too much," he cried. He tried to scream but there was no sound, only acceleration and black smoke. The flames and heat tore at his skin as he continued to fall. There was no bottom and his sense of time vanished. The feeling that he had now been falling for weeks or months filled his mind. Dread was upon him; fear was nothing compared to this hopelessness. Why was this happening? The depth of separation and abandonment was immense. He knew he would never see anyone again, not Linda, not anyone; he was made aware that he was utterly and eternally alone. *Oh God, where am I? Where are you?* he screamed in silence.

***

The ringing phone jarred him, his neck once again drenched. Dang this chair, he thought, it was haunted or something."

"Hello," he answered out of breath.

"Jeez, you okay?" Bud's voice greeted him.

"Yeah, yeah, fine. What's up, buddy? What you doin'; I saw your car," James said, quickly recovering.

"Oh, I see how it is; you saw my car but ignored me," Bud laughed.

"Yeah. No, not like that, bro. I was just doing some reading and I must have dozed off again. It's this stupid chair Doc gave me; I love it, but I can't stay awake in it."

"That happens to us older guys," Bud said. "I finished the outside lights; shouldn't be any more trouble," he added.

"You're too old to be working on stuff, Bud; you need to hire some help," James joked.

"Then I'll have to raise your rent," Bud said.

"Like I said, it's good for you to do these repairs, keeps you in the game," he said with a laugh.

"I'm outta here, James; I'll see you in church," Bud said.

"Okay, bro; thanks, goodnight."

He sat somewhat dumbfounded after he hung up. The nightmare was still fresh in his mind and it was unsettling to say the least. He got up and walked out the door to a brightly lit and smokeless hallway. He slowly walked to the stairs and looked down to the tile floor below. "Should have hit that in two seconds," he whispered.

Doubt and fear surrounded him for a minute before he identified the source and lifted his head and said, "Jesus, you are my rock, you are my fortress, in you I place my trust." He knew he was under attack and he was beginning to realize that it was constant. He thought that maybe the degree of spiritual attack was only mitigated by the strength of the Lord himself and that He determined what percentage of the attack actually reached a person. Maybe that's what it means by 'what was meant for evil will be used for good.' What if the spiritual warfare from the enemy was at a constant pitch all the time and it was God's filter that increased or decreased what anyone was facing at a given time?

There you go thinking again, you're the problem, he said to himself.

CHAPTER THIRTY

The preacher did a double take and then just stood and marveled at how beautiful this woman was. Her strawberry-blonde hair was braided with a lace-up leather band holding a ponytail. Black leather from head to toe and she stood there with her weight shifted to one side. Amazing. He thought he said, "wow," but wasn't sure if any sound came out.

"Did you forget you invited me to go for a ride this morning?" she asked.

"No, I was killing time waiting for you," he said.

"Oh please; I'm right on time," she said.

"Have you heard from Linda?" he asked.

She punched his arm and said, "Don't mess this up, mister; let's go for a ride."

Far be it from this preacher to second-guess or even try to figure out a woman's thinking but it did seem a bit of a stretch that Linda would one, jump on a bike with him and two, jump on a bike which would take the exact route that almost claimed his life a week earlier.

Let it be, the inner voice said.

Yeah, but didn't we just fight about this? he asked the voice.

Dude, let it go, the voice insisted.

Okay, but this is weird.

As manic as the previous couple of days had been, there was joy in Mudville that morning. With her arms wrapped around him, James felt whole. Linda felt safe. He patted her thigh as he readied the bike for a two-mile straightaway and then opened it up. He smiled when he heard her yell. What a great ride. Big Bear approached and with it the promise of a peaceful morning and a top-notch meal. James was excited to share his secret spot with Linda. After a giant breakfast of eggs, ham, hash browns, and fresh biscuits, they moved to the deck for another cup or two of coffee and to bask in the morning sunshine.

It was low sixties and the sun had no competition from any clouds. The sky at this elevation presented an almost translucent blue. The color appeared to be three-dimensional and go on forever. He leaned over and kissed her. She just looked at him with those green eyes and said, "I love you."

"Good," he said.

"So what's tonight's sermon, Preacher?"

"I have no idea, baby; it's been a weird week. I'll probably continue the spiritual warfare thread after I tell everyone Snake's amazing story." She looked at him quizzically. "Oh, I mean the healing part, not the CSI stuff," he laughed. She relaxed. "You want to walk around? There's a bunch of cool stores up here," he offered.

"Maybe later. You do what you have to do; I'm fine right here," she said.

Linda leaned back on two legs of her wooden chair an rested her long legs on the rustic railing that bordered the deck overlooking the busy street below. She sipped hot coffee and nibbled at a piece of banana nut bread. James was, as was his Saturday morning custom, pecking away at his laptop. He stole coffee from her cup when she looked away. Without saying a word they both hoped for many more Saturday mornings like this. Maybe, he thought, they could get a cabin up there someday. After all of the craziness, he absolutely loved the solitude of the mountains.

"Did you talk to Snake about your findings?" Linda's voice broke his trance.

"Yeah, last night," he said cautiously.

"How did it go?"

"Pretty good, I guess. He knows what I know at this point; now it's up to him."

"What do you think he's going to do?" she asked.

"I don't know; I really don't. There are several ways to handle things, obviously, but I promised you and Kit that I would back off and that's what I'm going to do," he said. "I will tell you that I'm glad I'm not Cedar right now," James said with a sly grin.

"Oh jeez, don't say it," she said, holding up her hand.

"He'll be better off if the cops get him before these guys," he said.

"If he's guilty, you mean?"

"Oh, of course. Hey, if he's innocent and this is all just the ramblings of an out-of-touch old outlaw, I'll deal with that, but there's too much evidence, albeit circumstantial, but I'd be surprised if we're wrong about this one," he said.

"Who's we?" she asked.

"Me and Gordon — Holmes and Watson," he laughed.

She smiled and slowly shook her head.

Another thirty minutes passed before James took his turn to break the silence. "Honey?"

Linda looked up. "Yes?"

"I would never involve you. I'm asking your advice on something I think the Lord is trying to tell me," he said.

"Well, if He's telling you something, why would you ask my advice?" she said.

"I think I need to warn Cedar somehow so he has a chance to escape," he said.

"Are you serious?" she asked. "After all you've done to prove his guilt?"

"I know, babe; I'm just thinking that the DMC will kill him and if I know that and let it happen, I'm an accessory. Maybe not legally, but morally. I can't look you or anyone else in the eye as a man of God knowing that I did nothing to stop it."

"Well, I know you're not a cop-caller, but maybe you need to let them know somehow before anything happens to him. Maybe he will go to jail for his part."

"The problem is they can't prove he did it. He can weasel out; any decent lawyer can prove reasonable doubt on this thing. If by some miracle of justice he goes to prison, they'll kill him there, they might even get to him in county before he gets transferred."

Linda just stared at him. "Wow, this stuff really happens, huh?"

"Yeah, honey, it really happens. The other thing is that I feel Snake is on the verge of coming to faith in Christ and the enemy is dragging him right back in. If he calls the shots on this, he's gonna go down sooner or later and that beef is a long one. It's like I can see what the devil is trying to orchestrate here; it's like a movie and I see Snake going down the wrong road and I can't say anything, but maybe I can get in front of it and prevent it."

James stared at the street below. "I almost didn't say anything to you about this, but then I realized that I have to; you're my wife … well almost … and I don't want to keep anything from you. This disagreement we had really kicked my butt. I've never had to consider anyone else, not since I joined the DMC, so it was easy for me to abide by the code of silence. I didn't have anyone, silence was second nature to me. People have been telling me secrets for as long as I can remember simply because they know I don't talk. I won't talk. I've got tons of issues, but gossip isn't one of them," he smiled.

"Well, just so you know, I hated fighting with you. I was just so scared; this is all very surreal to me at times. I love the Prophets and I actually kinda like Snake; I know how much he means to you. But that group, the DMC? They're animals and it sometimes scares me so much that I can't sleep knowing that you were an officer with them. I'm marrying you! My friends think I'm crazy, that this will pass, it's just a phase, an infatuation, but I know I am supposed to be with you. I know that God has called you to lead an amazing end times church and that the thrill of serving Him with you outweighs every fear I have, but let me tell you, this has stretched me *way* past my comfort zone!"

"Oh my gosh, me, too! I'm going to have to hang out with bankers. Do you know how that feels; do you know the nightmares I have?" he joked.

She socked him in the arm.

"Oww, you hit hard ... for a girl," he said and stopped and just stared at her. "I'm in love with you, Linda. I'm going to be a great husband and I'm going to strive to keep God at the forefront of our life together, I promise you that. I'm a little rough around the edges, I can be a little dark sometimes, but I'll always be here for you," he said.

"Oh, James, I love you, too. We're both going to have to adjust a bit, our lives are a bit of a contrast, but what we have I've never seen, not anywhere and my friends, they're just jealous becaise I got the big bad biker!"

CHAPTER THIRTY-ONE

He dialed Gordon's number hoping that the absent-minded professor had turned his phone on this particular Saturday night.

"Yes sir," Gordon answered, obviously responding to the caller I.D.

"Wassup, buddy?" the preacher asked.

"Not much. Getting ready to head your way; I like to get some coffee before service," Gordon answered.

"Yeah, and B.S. with Paige," James teased.

"Oh, yeah and that; I guess I don't hide that too well, huh?" Gordon asked.

"Not from a trained detective like myself," James joked. "Hey, did you call the paving company and leave that message?"

"Oh yeah, that was a little weird, but it worked out like we planned. I called from a pay phone off the 215 in San Bernardino. By the way, have you tried to find a pay phone lately? They are like gone, totally extinct, I swear. I found one like you said in a bad neighborhood;

thanks for that tip," Gordon laughed and then continued. "So I get this lady on the phone, like an answering service, so I made sure she could get a message to this Cedar character and she indicated that she could so I said, tell him the DMC and the MFers have called off the wedding, run or reap the whirlwind."

"She got that … you sure she got it like you said it?" James asked.

"I had her repeat it to me, it was verbatim," Gordon assured him.

"That should have him pretty constipated by now," James laughed.

"You did the right thing, James," Gordon said.

"Well, Gordon, we did what we could. None of this happens without you, bro; thanks for your tight lips. This is dead now," James said.

"Got ya, not a problem. Oh, I dropped the big envelope in the mail like you asked, no return address; it's enough to build a case if they ever find the guy," Gordon added.

"Cool, our work here is finished," James said.

CHAPTER THIRTY-TWO

James answered the knock on his office door. "Preacher, sorry to bother you, bro; I know this is your time but there's some lady downstairs who says she's your sister."

James slowly got up from the couch, carefully folded his notes inside his Bible, and placed it on the coffee table. He looked at his friend Flip, a long-time Prophet and said, "Well, I guess you should send her up. Did she mention her name?" James joked.

"Dude, you don't know your own sister's name?" Flip asked.

"Just kidding, bro; it's Denise or Diane or something like that. It's been awhile, but I'm sure it'll come to me."

Flip just shook his head and headed downstairs to help his brother out.

James would have trotted down the stairs and greeted her himself, but he needed the couple of minutes to gather his wits. He searched his mind to remember when he last saw his little sister.

"Michelle's funeral," she said, coming through the door.

"Huh … what?" he asked.

"The last time we saw each other," she said.

"Oh, I guess so. What … I mean … how … why … how did you find me?" the preacher asked.

"Nice to see you, too," she joked.

James hugged her and said, "I'm sorry. I'm happy to see you; it's just a big surprise."

"*You're* surprised?" she asked. "My outlaw biker convict brother is a pastor," she cried.

"You have a point," he laughed. "But really, how did you find me?"

"I googled you," she laughed.

"Shut up," he said.

"No kidding, I really did," she said. "I have a girlfriend who told me about your church and I couldn't believe it so I googled you."

"So I'm on Google; who knew?" he said.

"I know, right?" she said.

"You want some coffee? I have iced tea and some Perrier or regular bottled water," he asked.

"Is the coffee ready? I don't want you to make it just for me," she said.

"Oh, I've got the coolest coffee gadget ever made, don't you worry. Check it out," he said, waving her toward the kitchen area of his office.

"It's nice here. I like the office; this just for you?" she asked.

"Yeah, I have it set up how I like it, I spend a lot of time up here, mostly evenings and for sure a couple of hours on Saturday before service. You're staying for the service, I hope?" he asked.

"Yes, I plan on it," she said.

James took out the *Aeropress* and created a piping hot single cup of amazing coffee in about two minutes.

"How do you like it?" he asked.

"Sugar only," she said.

"You always liked your sugar," he said. "Hey, you remember Linda, the bank manager where you set up my account when I was in prison?"

"Sure do, the pretty one. I think I mentioned that in my letter to you," she said.

"We're getting married," he said.

"Shut the front door!" she cried. "You're serious? How awesome. Oh my gosh, really? Oh James, oh wow, really?

"Yes, what's so hard to believe?" he joked. "I mean aside from the fact that she's beautiful and successful and I'm ... me."

"You're definitely you, but that's not all bad, evidently. Things have certainly changed for you, no?" she commented.

"Yeah, you could say that," he said.

"You'll have to fill me in on all of this," she said.

"Only if you fill me in on you, too," he replied and sent a text to Linda, asking her to come upstairs for a surprise.

"Well, okay, but my life is boring compared to yours," she added.

"Really? Something brought you to me, sis; you'll need to fill me in later," he said.

"You sure you want to hear my drama?" she asked.

"Oh yeah, drama is my specialty."

***

"Come on in," James said in response to the gentle knock on the normally trespass-free office door.

"What's the surprise?" she said as she walked through the doorway.

"Remember my sister, Diane?"

"Oh my gosh!" Linda squealed. "How nice to see you! What a nice surprise. Did you know your sister was coming?" she turned and asked James, as if Diane wasn't there.

"Nope, but a nice surprise," he said.

The two women shared a "church" hug and began the small talk one would expect from two people thrown into an uncomfortable social situation.

Especially when their host wandered off to finish his notes for the upcoming sermon.

"Honey, Diane and I are going downstairs to get our seats. Are you all set; you need anything?" Linda asked.

James looked up distractedly, as if the two ladies had just walked in on him. "Huh, oh sure, no, I'm good, babe. Thanks, sorry, I was preoccupied ... hey Diane, when did you get here?" he joked.

"Ha ha," she said. "Okay, brother, I'll see you on stage. Nice to see you again."

"Likewise; we should hang out more often, sis. Hey, where's your ol' man?" he asked.

"Oh … um … he's with some work friends. I'll get him to come out some other time," she said.

"Look forward to it; we'll hang out after service tonight if you can stay. The afterglow is pretty fun around here," James said.

"I look forward to it," she said and gave him a hug.

Linda kissed him quickly and the two headed out the door.

CHAPTER LAST

He could make out the beginning of "God of Wonders" in the big room downstairs, grabbed his Bible, and headed out to the stairs. He wondered if there would come a time where he would view that stairway normally or would that nightmare always cloud his mind.

He timed his stage entrance perfectly and took a long appreciative look at the room full of people. He always saw new faces each week, a sign of healthy growth, as everyone was there by word of mouth. He considered advertising, but found that a handful of business cards and a group of friendly people could do more for church growth than any other medium. These people loved it here and he knew of their commitment. They were a 'down' congo, as Stewart would say.

"Hey, praise the Lord everyone. How you all doing tonight?" he yelled. The audience responded with loud applause and some whistles. "You guys clean up pretty nice," he said. "No, I'm serious. God just showed me a snapshot of you when I walked out here and I just realized how much I appreciate every one of you. I pray

God's blessings on you all and that His will is manifested in each of our lives. Amen?" he said. The crowd responded, more like exploded with cheers and applause. This would be a great night.

"You guys all know that our friend Snake had a bad wreck last week and I rushed out of here after service. I apologize, by the way, if I was short or rude with anyone; I was in a panic and, well, they were going to pull the plug on him early Sunday morning," he said and paused for effect. The congregation was quiet and hanging on his words. "Well, check it out. God had other plans for Snake because he's going home on Monday and the doctors are freaking out!"

Surprised mayhem might describe the joy that overtook the audience. People were hugging each other and high-fiving others two and three rows back. James just let them run with it for a good minute or so before bringing the room back to sanity. "You guys, I'm tellin you that what happened over there was so huge, we got to minister to Snake's parents; the doctors and nurses got a taste of our God and His power. Amen?" and the crowd went wild again.

This time James used both hands to bring the place to order. "So we're just gonna be happy, we're gonna believe that God can do anything, that with Him all things are possible."

As sometimes happened, the sermon he'd written earlier was changed at the point of delivery. He loved when the Spirit of God messed with him like that. It kept the natural order of things ... in order. The preacher knew that it he availed himself to God, kept himself humble and teachable, God would use him and it was times like these that lit his spiritual fuse. "I was going to talk a bit more tonight about spiritual warfare and trials and tribulations but I have a feeling that He," James rolled his eyes upward, lifting his head slightly, "has other plans." The room laughed and yelled out praise for the Lord.

"Someone very close to me who's not very close to me came to see me today," James started. "She reminded me without saying anything that we need to "Seek first the kingdom of God and His righteousness and all these things will be added to us." He paused. "Amen?" he asked.

"Amen," they answered.

"You know that we chase the wrong things for the wrong reason all day long right?" He was preachin' now. "You know we chase relationships to make *us* feel good, not the other person; you know we chase power and prestige and fame and money and position so that other people will think we *are* all that?

"You know that we are all selfish, well, all except Linda; she's all about making me happy," he said amidst laughter and catcalls. Linda looked at him with the, *you will pay for this later* look that he loved so much. "We all live like this to varying degrees; don't look at me like that! This is human nature; this is why the word says to seek first the kingdom of God, seek God first and then God will take care of our needs."

James took a long pull from his 'thirty-three degree' bottle of Perrier, the only thing he'd walk to the edge of the stage for during a sermon.

"Oh, that's good," he said as the carbonation made him shake his head. "You remember the old Jackie Gleason shows? Don't play dumb with me, Oh jeez,

Bud, you remember Jackie Gleason! Remember how he would sit and have his coffee and make that Whoaaa sound when he drank it? That's how this stuff works for me; work with me here," he said to laughter.

"So I says to myself the other night as I'm reading the Bible — cause you know I'm ultra spiritual — while you're out riding motorcycles or bowling or watching movies or softball of whatever people like you do, I am reading the Bible getting ready for you guys on Saturday night!" Linda covered her eyes at that. He was in a wonderful mood and having a ball with his congregation tonight. "This is the joy of the Lord. Amen?" he said.

More laughter and "Amens" throughout the room.

"Anyway, quit interrupting me. Anyway, as I'm going over this passage I realized that God could very well have already done all these cool things for us and they are just waiting to be triggered by our obedience to His admonition here. It's like faith; it's impossible to please God without faith and it's kinda tough to be obedient without faith, too. You can fake it for awhile, that's what the legalists do, but you can't live it. So, like dominoes, 'all these things' are in a holding pattern just waiting for us to seek God. As we seek Him, the cool things God has for us start falling into our lives. Like a plan. Like maybe God's plan? Like maybe that's God's will for us, seeking Him? Ya think?

"I used to think it was like, 'You do this and God will do that,' like some kind of game or something, but that puts us in the driver's seat, that's the enemy again. Remember what we said about initiating and responding, God has to be the initiator, so it makes sense in light of scripture that says we've already been given all we need for life and godliness, that 'all these things' would be included in the 'already been given everything we need for life and godliness,' so as we seek God, this stuff lines up in our lives and we are in synch.

"Our faith only accesses the things that God has already positioned for us. Our faith does not cause God to do anything. If you remember only one thing from tonight, let that be it. He initiates, we respond; if you've got that flipped around, you are in error.

"So again, instead of scheming and planning and manipulating people and time and events to suit some selfish intention, let's try starting our day with, 'Here am I, Lord, your will be done, guide me and teach me, live your life through me.' You see the difference here, that's faith, that's trust. What are we afraid of? What is our major malfunction here? Maybe we don't trust that God has a better plan. We don't trust God. Simple as that."

James looked out and caught his sister and Linda in the second row. "I'm not talking about you, sis; don't trip on me," he said. "Everyone, my sister Diane is in the house. Stand up, baby sister, say hi to everyone," he teased. The cheers of several hundred people greeted Diane as she reluctantly stood and took her bow. She shook her finger at her brother as she sat down. "It's really good to have you here, sis.

"You know the more I preach on this the more I realize we should devote at least another week to this teaching. Faith is everything. The Bible says without faith it's impossible to please God and I don't know about you, but if we're going to ride this horse, we should ride it to win. I mean if we're in this for the right reasons, we should want God to be pleased, right?"

The congo agreed loudly.

The preacher continued. " I mean, do we want God's will for our lives or do we want our will for our lives? Do we want our prayers answered or do we want God's will for our lives? You see what I'm saying? God has a better plan; why don't we trust Him? We think we have a better plan, that's why. It's that simple; we dumb humans are convinced that we have a better plan," he laughed. "I'm not laughing at you; I'm just as guilty of this as anyone!" he cried. "We all do this; what the heck is wrong with us?"

"Again, I said faith is everything, but it's got to be the right faith; we have to have the right mindset about faith. Faith is not a tool to get God to do what we want Him to do. Amen?"

The crowd agreed.

"You say amen, but what's our prayer life all about? Oh God, please give me … fill in the blank: that job, that spouse, that boyfriend, those lottery numbers 'cause you know you can trust me with the money, God," he said to laughter. "We need to grow to the point where we can ask for whatever we ask for, but end it with 'Your will be done,' and mean it. Jesus himself, when faced with unimaginable stress in the garden of Gethsemane said, 'Nevertheless, your will not mine be done.'"

If Jesus was to the point of asking for something but stuck that 'your will be done' on the end of His prayer, shouldn't we? He's God, for crying out loud, but He did nothing without the Father's go-ahead. He didn't say or do anything that wasn't of the Father. Now we're not Jesus, but His example is staring us in the face and I'm thinkin' we need to take notes here. Jesus didn't run His own program, He was always praying and seeking His Father's will. He said it many times; 'I only do what the Father tells me.' What? You mean, you don't just run off thinking your idea is the end all? Remember the scripture that says, 'Don't say we're going to this town or that town and we're going to do this and that and make money, rather say, 'If God allows, we will do this and that.'

"That's what I'm talking about here. We need to stop and realize who is running this show and it's not us! Or it shouldn't be us, but it's always us; we're always leaning on our own understanding. Nobody seeks God the way we're supposed to, its human nature; we've all been raised to take charge. How many of you were raised by someone who said, 'If you want something done right you've got to do it yourself?'

"Faith in Him is what we need. Not faith in our faith or faith in thinking we can change God's mind if enough of us ask for something. Oh, my prayers aren't enough, I'll get the prayer team to bring it to God and if that's not enough, I'll get my email list praying; that'll surely work. I'll ask you again and I want you to think about this: Do we want our prayers answered or do we want God's will for our lives?"

Again the crowd reacted emotionally and enthusiastically. The preacher knew that it would be short-lived — it was like a multi-level sales meeting right now — but at least he got them off the fence for a short time tonight. Maybe some of this would stick, somebody would 'get it.'

He noticed a commotion in the back and several people standing up; some were moving chairs. Soon, everyone was turned to see what was going on. The preacher tried to discern the issue — it wasn't entirely unheard of to have altercations on occasion. Such was the risk of allowing anyone and everyone to attend this place, but this didn't look like a fight; it was orderly. Still, there was quite a buzz in the back of the room. James stopped and waited. He glanced at his usual sentries, but they were already moving toward the back of the room.

"It's him; it's Snake," a voice said.

James could hear the room begin to erupt in praise and sounds of laughter as Mike and Sylvia Vandermere rolled the wheelchair down the aisle and dozens of Doomsayers, all with arms crossed at the waist in respect, filled the back wall. From her front row seat, Linda looked at James and covered her mouth, tears filling her eyes. She was not alone.

The preacher stepped down from the stage and shook Mike's hand and hugged Sylvia and then lightly hugged Snake's shoulder, taking care not to touch his bandaged head. "You're early," he said to Snake.

"Oh, I wasn't quite as sick as I let on," he said, quoting Doc Holliday from their favorite late-night movie, *Tombstone*.

"You're good for business around here," Preacher said. "People are starting to believe that with God, anything is possible."

"I came for one reason, bro, and then I'm outta here till I get better. I came here to show respect the only way I know how."

Preacher took the microphone and held it in front of Snake's mouth. The damaged giant closed his eyes and reached for these words: "I ... we, my family, the club ... we just wanted you to know how much we appreciate your kindness, your prayer ... your friendship."

The crowd murmured their response, many people crying openly, several folks yelling out, "Praise the Lord," and "we love you, Snake," before Snake said, "I'll be back soon. We have much to do together. God bless you all."

This time there was no murmuring, just a spontaneous standing ovation, which lasted while he was being wheeled back up the long aisle and out the door. Magic walked down to the preacher and hugged him long and hard and publicly before he led his patch holders out the door after their president.

There was no sign of Cedar.

About the Author:

John Andrews lives in Southern California with his wife DeEtt. When he's not writing Outlaw Preacher adventures he's on his boat attempting to catch fish (he can't catch fish) off the coast of San Diego or managing Promised Land Express, Inc, a refrigerated trucking company with offices in S. Cal and N. Texas. He also founded TKO-Trust, Know, One Christian clothing. Check out: www.tkostore.com for some edgy designs. John is a charter member of The Prophets MC in So. Cal. Check out the club (yes, they are real) at: www.prophetsmc91.com

Please join our crew at: www.theoutlawpreacher.com and check out the Outlaw gear.

CPSIA information can be obtained at www.ICGtesting.com
Printed in the USA
LVOW101324270613

340538LV00005B/11/P